Blessed Invasion

Liberating an Occupied Planet

Blessed Invasion

Liberating an Occupied Planet

Wallace Henley

Take note that the name satan and related names are not capitalized. We choose not to acknowledge him, even to the point of violating grammatical rules.

Treasure House

An Imprint of

Destiny Image® Publishers, Inc.
P.O. Box 310
Shippensburg, PA 17257-0310

"For where your treasure is,
there will your heart be also." Matthew 6:21

ISBN 1-56043-196-2

For Worldwide Distribution
Printed in the U.S.A.

This book and all other Destiny Image, Revival Press, and Treasure House books are available at Christian bookstores and distributors worldwide.

For a U.S. bookstore nearest you, call **1-800-722-6774**.
For more information on foreign distributors,
call **717-532-3040**.
Or reach us on the Internet: **http://www.reapernet.com**

Dedication

This book is dedicated to Charles and Sharon Carroll of Singapore, valiant warriors in the Kingdom advance who have been sifted and now are strengthening the brothers and sisters everywhere.

Acknowledgments

Undertaking a project like *Blessed Invasion* drives one rapidly into the hard wall of his own limitations. Without a lot of help, no one can surmount the obstacles of his own fallibility. I have received such help, and without it this book would not now be in your hands.

I acknowledge the ministry of the Holy Spirit. It will be up to the reader to discern just how clearly I have heard the Lord. But I have written here ideas and concepts that my limited grasp of history could not know without the revelatory work of the Spirit of God. Where there is accuracy and impartation, the praise goes to Him.

I must also acknowledge the special role of my wife. Irene is a courageous trouper who walks the world with me, even when boarding another airplaine seems less desirable than a root canal. She was with me that day in Normandy when God changed my worldview. Her discernment has blasted away my smoggy confusion many times.

I am blessed to serve a church that understands my call to travel and write. The Encourager Church staff, elders, and people are folk of remarkable vision and faith. I am indebted to them beyond my ability to repay, and count it one of the great blessings of life to be joined with them.

Working with the Destiny Image team has been an extraordinary blessing. Rare is the publishing house that is driven more by a passion for truth than for the bottom line, by the call to be a prophet more than the desire to make a profit. Don Nori has poured apostolic vision into Destiny Image. Don Milam has encouraged me with his dedication to helping authors maximize the impact of the message God gives them. Elizabeth Allen is a marvelous communicator who links author and process so that the integrity of the message is maintained. I thank also Stephen Nance for sharpening my prose and bringing the central themes into clear focus.

May the Lord use *Blessed Invasion* to bring new fire to the vision of the Church of Jesus Christ, to drive back the invader, and to restore the world to its rightful owner—our Father.

Wallace Henley

Endorsements

"I am more than a little impressed with Wallace Henley's latest book. He combines excellent historical research with spiritual insight to produce a captivating exposition of the Kingdom."

—Paul Cain

"*Blessed Invasion* is an articulate, stimulating explanation of the advance of the Kingdom of Christ, and an inspiring call to Christians to take their place in Christ's army."

—Dr. Jack Deere

"Having migrated into the peaceful valleys of political correctness, the elders of modern Christianity have distanced themselves from battlefield metaphors and analogies. The terminology is simply too confrontational.

"In *Blessed Invasion* Wallace Henley resists this trend—emphatically. Using terms like beachhead, stronghold, and liberation—biblical concepts all—he reminds us that we have been called to war against the powers of sin and darkness. And the battle is already here!

"Although he pulls no punches in his description of contemporary humanist and occult forces, Henley is optimistic about our chances. Since God has enlightened and empowered us, we need not shrink in fear. This is our hour, not the enemy's."

—George Otis, Jr.

Wallace Henley has written a truly remarkable book. His weaving together of the history of World War II and some of its major military and political lessons with the need for Christians to spiritually liberate our planet from its oppressors is truly extraordinary. It should be obvious that only a history buff and pastor-theologian who has a background in the world of public policy and strategic thinking could have written this book. My advice to you, the reader, is simple: Take your time, drink deeply, and pray as you go!

—Dennis Peacocke

Contents

Preface

A Normandy Parable

Herve and Michelle DuPree lived in a small house beside the narrow highway between Arromanche and Ste. Mere-Eglise. Now in their seventies and too old to farm, they subsisted on the milk from one worn-out cow and on the vegetables they grew in a small garden plot.

Nazi soldiers sometimes banged on the door, demanding food. Michelle would bring them bread and soup, making sure to spit in the soup when they weren't looking. Sometimes they forced Herve to milk the cow.

One summer morning Herve heard thunder. The weather had been bad over the English Channel, so he went outside to look for the storm. The booming sounds continued, however, shaking the ground beneath him. Turning around, he saw cracks appearing between the stone blocks of the old house where he and his family had lived for generations. He rushed back to the house to rescue Michelle before the building collapsed. They waited nervously in the yard, but the house remained standing.

Then they heard the rumbling of heavy engines. It seemed as though every German soldier from the direction of Bayeux and Caen was pouring down to the coastline. Convoy after convoy passed by. Herve and Michelle went inside and hurried up the narrow stairs into their bedroom, which overlooked the road. Throwing the shutters open, they watched the armies pass.

For what seemed an eternity, they listened to the rumbling and thundering coming from the coast. Then a strange reversal took place. Dazed, dirty, and weary German soldiers and fragments of convoys passed by their window again, only this time moving inland. The flow of retreating troops diminished steadily until, finally, there were no more. For an hour there was an eerie silence.

Then, from the direction of the coast came the deep-throated rumble of engines. Herve pondered a moment, then shouted to Michelle, "Go gather some onions, and make soup!"

"Shall I spit in it?" his wife asked.

"No, make it your best," Herve replied. "Our liberators are approaching!"

Within half an hour the leading edge of the Allied landing force entered the village. Herve and Michelle stood on their doorstep embracing each other and dancing as the first American convoy came into view. One of the vehicles stopped in front of the house. An officer leaped out and approached Herve.

"I'm afraid we'll need this house to establish a perimeter," he said through an interpreter.

Herve nodded.

The officer looked up at the bedroom window, "With a machine gun in that window, we can sweep the whole street."

Michelle listened quietly. The bedroom was where she had birthed her four children on her mother's antique bed. That didn't matter. The liberators could have the room.

"Are you hungry?" Herve asked the officer. "My wife has made soup…we have bread and wine…I have even milked my cow!"

Herve and Michelle withheld nothing of theirs from their liberators. For them, it was a *blessed invasion.*

Foreword

I realized as I sat down to pen a word about this book that I seldom buy a book because of its title. I place a great deal of stock in a "credible witness." This book confirms that principle.

Wallace Henley, formerly in the Nixon White House inner circle, is a great thinker, statesman, and speaker. His writing is what I call "fetching"; that is, it demands further reading. When you read one of his works, you will vow that the remainder of them are "must reads!"

For those many of us who at times wonder what in the world is going on, this book forms a most profitable text. Those who do not properly interpret history sentence themselves to ignorance regarding current events. With that ignorance will come a sense of futility, if not carelessness.

Henley's reading on the past sharpens his awareness of the pressing issues of the present and their bearing on the future. His anticipation about the future brings fresh hope to souls wearied with bad news. His evaluation for the present brings the reader pleasure to be alive. As I read it first for the purpose of evaluation, I had trouble laying it down and since have used the manuscript for some research of my own writing projects.

This book will have a long, profitable, and productive life. It is a book that will make you think and at the same time make you glad to be alive at this time in history. It is a welcome fresh breath of literary air in a world filled with a great deal of literary carbon dioxide. It is a book that will have you standing on tiptoes with excitement and bending knees in grateful prayer for the prospect of the planet being shaken by a loving God back to its senses until only that which is unshakable remains.

Jack Taylor
Dimensions Minstries
Melbourne, FL

Introduction

Now having been questioned by the Pharisees as to when the kingdom of God was coming, He answered them and said, "The kingdom of God is not coming with signs to be observed; nor will they say, 'Look, here it is!' or, 'There it is!' For behold, the kingdom of God is in your midst." (Luke 17:20-21)

"History," said Henry Ford, "is bunk." Thomas Carlyle was only slightly more gracious when he wrote, "History is a distillation of rumor." Even during the Enlightenment of the eighteenth and nineteenth centuries, cynicism abounded. "The history of the great events of the world is little more than a history of crime," moaned Voltaire. Oliver Goldsmith agreed, saying that the history of Europe, at least, was little more than "a tissue of crimes, follies, and misfortunes."

Such pessimism is characteristic of humanity's view of much of its past. It is a view from the bottom up, beginning with the muck and mire of disillusionment, meaninglessness, and hopelessness. It is no surprise, then, that modern social prophets see mankind's future as equally dismal. Samuel Huntington foresees a "clash of civilizations," Robert Kaplan "a coming anarchy," and Paul Friedman "a day of reckoning."

There is, however, another view of history, one that sees the "big picture" from the top down, a view that offers hope to humanity. The Bible views natural, observed, and experienced phenomena as types and symbols of core reality. The natural world *is* real. The biblical worldview, however, rejects both the Eastern mystical belief in *maya*—that the natural world is unreal illusion—and the Western rationalistic view that human experience of reality is all the reality there is. Creation is much greater than the sum of its biological, mechanical, and material parts.

Creation is a statement. The natural world tells us something *important*. It is not surprising that the Bible reveals the act of creation as *word*. God *said*, and all things came into being. As the psalmist said, "The heavens are telling of the glory of God; and their expanse is declaring the work of His hands."[1]

This same worldview is found in the New Testament. The apostle Paul states that everyone is accountable to God. Even those who have had no direct experience of God still have the revelation of nature: For since creation, God's "invisible attributes, His eternal power and divine

1. Psalm 19:1.

nature, have been clearly seen, being understood through what has been made, so that they are without excuse."[2]

First Corinthians 15 contains a key principle for understanding the relationship of the natural world to the supernatural world. Paul contrasts the physical body to the spiritual being, writing, "...the spiritual is not first, but the natural; then the spiritual."[3] The natural is observed first in the physical world, but always undergirding it is the spiritual. The natural is not illusion, nor is it disconnected from reality. Full reality encompasses both the natural and the supernatural. The temporal rises from the eternal, the physical from the spiritual.

There is, then, a correlation between the natural and the spiritual. Just as all objects in nature are subject to the law of gravity, with denser bodies pulling lighter ones "downward" toward them, there is "gravity" in the spiritual realm also. Because of the entry of sin, all creation is being pulled "downward," toward hell, from the order of God's *cosmos*, to the disorder of *chaos*. Another correlation is the law of displacement. Just as dense matter displaces lighter matter, so the Kingdom of God displaces the kingdom of darkness.

Natural creation tells the story of this reality, and the theme is the Kingdom of God. Human history, as a facet of creation, makes a statement about this reality. The profile of spiritual realities can be seen in historical events.

---

2. Romans 1:20.
3. 1 Corinthians 15:46.

It is the thesis of this book that the Normandy invasion of Europe in World War II is a profound statement about the battle for the destiny of the "first heaven," creation—where humanity is to have "dominion"—between the "Third Heaven," the Kingdom of God, and the "second heaven," the realm of satan and the kingdom of chaos and darkness.

When the Allied invasion force appeared off the beaches of Normandy on the morning of June 6, 1944, the German defenders were taken completely by surprise. The weather was too poor for an invasion. Field Marshal Erwin Rommel, who was in command of the shore defenses along the Normandy coast, was in Germany for his wife's birthday. Many other high-ranking German officers were away on leave also. Hitler himself, tucked away in his Alpine retreat, wasn't even wakened when the Normandy landings began. Little did he know that, despite many battles yet to come, *he was defeated the moment the Allies set foot on European soil.*

The Allies had a clear objective. General Dwight D. Eisenhower, the Supreme Allied Commander in Europe, had received a simple, direct order: "You will enter the Continent of Europe and...undertake operations aimed at the heart of Germany and the destruction of her armed forces." Every subsequent plan and strategy was aimed at accomplishing this.

Two thousand years ago the Ally of the human race and the Liberator of occupied earth landed on the planet. At Omaha Beach on D-Day, the breakthrough was made by a few foot soldiers scurrying off the battered beach toward the slopes beyond—not an auspicious beginning for the liberation of a continent. So, too, the coming of Jesus seemed a small, insignificant event. The Liberator had come, whether He was recognized or not. His orders were as simple as those received by Eisenhower. The Father instructed the Son to restore His original intent in creation: Get it back, fill it with God's glory, and liberate the entire universe.

By the end of July 1944, 1.5 million Allied soldiers were in France, fighting their way to Germany. In like manner, the first task Jesus faced was filling the occupied world with His people. His basic objective was to restore *zoe*, or "spirit life," to the sin-oppressed world. This restoration of spirit-life was to God's divine strategy what the invasion of Allied forces was to the liberation of Europe.

In the Garden of Eden, God had warned Adam not to eat the fruit of the forbidden tree, lest he die.[4] Adam disobeyed and immediately died spiritually. His *zoe* left him, leaving only his *bios*, or physical life, and even that began the process toward death and decay.

Jesus is the second "Adam." He came to earth in a *bios* body, experienced all the pain and limitations of human existence, then was crucified and buried. Three days later, He rose, free of *bios*, and alive once more with pure *zoe*. He has the power to give His *zoe* to all who will receive Him.

But now Christ has been raised from the dead, the first fruits of those who are asleep. For since by a man came death, by

---

4. Genesis 2:17.

a man also came the resurrection of the dead. For as in Adam all die, so also in Christ all shall be made alive. ... So also it is written, "The first man, Adam, became a living soul." The last Adam became a life-giving spirit (1 Corinthians 15:20-22,45).

When Jesus came in the flesh, He not only restored spirit-life, but also established the Kingdom of God on the earth. By the end of D-Day, the Allies had established a foothold on French soil, not to be dislodged. From that moment, the ultimate defeat of Germany was only a matter of time. With the coming of Jesus, the final defeat of satan and his realm is only a matter of time.

The Kingdom of God is not a future hope, but a present reality because it is in Jesus Himself. He came to destroy the works of the oppressor.[5] His Kingdom of peace stands against satan's kingdom and the chaos it brings. The Kingdom of God displaces the kingdom of darkness.

Andre Mace, a citizen of the little Normandy town of Ste. Mere Eglise, witnessed the Allied invasion. He proclaimed that scores of paratroopers "are landing everywhere amid gunfire...our liberators are here!"

The deliverance of occupied earth has come down from Heaven. Our Liberator is here! He has come in a blessed invasion. *And it is here now.*

---

5. 1 John 3:8.

Chapter 1

"Welcome to Our Liberators"

Welcome to Our Liberators read the signs on the walls of battered old farm buildings, weary village shops, schools, houses, and everywhere else a flat surface could be found.

My wife, Irene, and I were touring the Normandy region of France in 1995. The year before, the region had celebrated the fiftieth anniversary of the D-Day landings of June 6, 1944. Battle veterans from many countries, along with their families, had marched through the area once more, remembering and celebrating.

The older people of Normandy remembered how the Allied troops had demolished their villages, shredded their carefully cultivated fields with tanks and artillery, and used their homes and church towers as gun emplacements. They also recalled how delighted they had been to give whatever they had to help the Allies defeat the Nazis. Despite great personal risk, the French in Normandy had welcomed the D-Day assault because, for those chafing under the Nazi boot, it was a blessed invasion.

That day the Lord reminded me of another strategic French beach of the war—Dunkirk. There, in May and June, 1940, four British divisions and the French First Army found themselves trapped with their backs to the sea. They had escaped destruction by the Germans through a miraculous rescue.

On May 10, Hitler had swept into neutral Belgium with an unprecedented armored force and smashed through the center of the French line. The British First Army Group had left their own fortifications and moved into Belgium to help defend the line.

The German advance proceeded with such speed that by May 25 all communications with the British and French armies in Belgium had been severed, the escape route to the south had been cut off by the Nazis, and King Leopold of Belgium was about to step down. Britain's sole hope depended on the escape of her armies.

Winston Churchill and his War Cabinet knew the only possibility of saving the armies was to pull them northward to the English Channel. It would not be easy. There was the danger that the retreating armies would become surrounded and be destroyed. Nevertheless, Lord Gort, commander of the British forces, decided to establish a beachhead at Dunkirk.

At this point Hitler was concerned that his forces would get mired in the low, canal-laced country, and he was confident that his air force could stop the evacuation of the

British and their allies. Hitler ordered General Halder, Chief of the German General Staff, to stop the pursuit. Miraculously, the path to Dunkirk suddenly opened up before the British.

Still, the Germans continued to press on the Belgian front to the south. The Belgian army, which had valiantly held back the German advance, finally capitulated. The German armies, no longer concerned about getting bogged down, poured through the gap opened by the Belgian collapse. At 1:00 p.m. on May 27, the British War Office sent Lord Gort an order: "Evacuate the maximum force possible."

In the days that followed, Churchill's government scoured Britain for anything that would float. Hundreds of tugs and other small boats, 11 destroyers, 14 mine sweepers, and 40 French and Belgian craft evacuated the warriors from Dunkirk. On June 4, 1940, the British Admiralty announced the completion of "Operation Dynamo," that 338,000 British and Allied soldiers were safely in England.

Two days and four years later, another beachhead in northern France, Normandy, would signal the end for Hitler and his regime. For now, though, Britain stood alone against Germany.

* * *

A half century later, the human race is approaching another beachhead of sorts, the twenty-first century. An uncertain world faces the future with many questions. Opinions are voiced, books written, and analyses rendered.

Zbigniew Brzezinski, former White House national security adviser, observing this looming beachhead, wrote of the coming "global turmoil" in the twenty-first century in his book *Out of Control*.[1] The twentieth century began with the hope and optimism that the fruits of the Industrial Revolution would produce a techno-paradise. Reason would govern in a stable world. Yet today, many approach the twenty-first century with apprehension, dread, and hopelessness. Paul Kennedy, in *Preparing for the Twenty-First Century*, writes that "as the Cold War fades away, we face not a 'new world order' but a troubled and fractured planet, whose problems deserve the serious attention of politicians and publics alike."[2]

The promise of the twentieth century was blown to pieces when the brilliant gadgets that had sparked optimism became instruments of destruction, producing what Brzezinski calls a "century of megadeath." Technical and scientific progress, he says, "was not matched on the moral level."[3] In fact, "the twentieth century became mankind's most bloody and hateful century, a century of hallucinatory politics and of monstrous killings."[4] Above all else, the twentieth century is one in which humanity "sought to *usurp the divine* and was cast into an apocalypse of his own making."[5]

1. Zbigniew Brzezinski, *Out of Control* (New York: Charles Scribner's Sons, 1993).
2. Paul Kennedy, *Preparing for the Twenty-First Century* (New York: Random House, 1993), 349.
3. Brzezinski, *Out of Control*, 4.
4. Brzezinski, *Out of Control*, 4.
5. Brzezinski, *Out of Control*, 44, emphasis added.

Anxiety and anticipation are the dueling moods as man faces the future. The anxious are those who look at the beachhead of the twenty-first century and conclude we've arrived at Dunkirk. Those who look ahead with anticipation see it as Normandy. Sadly, many in the Church have bought into the "Dunkirk" mentality. They expect to dig in and hang on until they are taken away. Others see the twenty-first century as a beachhead of opportunity; these persons are preparing to land, occupy, and advance to the last stronghold of the enemy. The "Dunkirk" view focuses on escape, while the "Normandy" view focuses on opportunity and authority.

There are, then, both "Dunkirk" and "Normandy" people in the Church. It is important to understand the distinctions between the two:

"Dunkirk" is surprised by enemy attack, while "Normandy" specializes in surprising the enemy. The British and their Allies were shocked at Germany's sweep through Belgium and had to flee to safety. It was quite the other way on June 6, 1944. The Normandy invasion was a complete surprise to the Germans. The church with the "Dunkirk" mentality is caught off guard by the blitz of the destroyer. So, it focuses primarily on rescue and escape.

The "Normandy" view, on the other hand, is one of advance until victory is complete. Ste. Mere-Eglise is a small town in Normandy that was liberated by American paratroopers. A citizen of Ste. Mere-Eglise asked an American soldier, Lt. James Coyle, if the assault was a raid or the invasion. "*Nous restons ici,*" replied Lt. Coyle, "we are staying here."[6] So the "Normandy" church has staying power because she has clear focus on her mission.

The "Dunkirk" church adopts a defeatist attitude toward battle with the enemy. When the Allied armies were trapped at Dunkirk, many feared that the war was as good as over—with Germany as the victor. The "Normandy" church, on the other hand, is confident of victory. Although the enemy may mount strong counter-offensives, such efforts are merely the dying gasps of a defeated foe. As the Allies advanced deeper into Europe in late 1944, Hitler launched a daring and desperate counter-strike. The Battle of the Bulge threatened to halt or reverse the Allied advance. The Allied leaders, however, refused to give in to a defeatist mentality, and the German attack failed. So, despite the attacks and effort of the enemy, the "Normandy" church knows that victory is assured.

Thus, Dunkirk is retreat, but Normandy is advance. Teddy Roosevelt, son of the famed American president, was an officer helping lead the Normandy assault. His unit, like many others, landed at the wrong place. When he became aware of the error, General Roosevelt said, "We'll start the war from right here!"

There are additional characteristics that distinguish the "Dunkirk" church from the "Normandy" church.

The "Dunkirk" Mentality in the Church

One characteristic of the "Dunkirk" church is that it drifts away from the simple teaching of Jesus and the basics of apostolic doctrine, which results in a distorted vision of

6. Brzezinski, *Out of Control*, 313.

the enemy. It falls into one or the other of the extremes described by C.S. Lewis in *The Screwtape Letters*: Either it comes to disbelieve in the existence of the devil and his demons on the one hand, or it is grasped by an "excessive" and "unhealthy" interest in them on the other, focusing so much on the devil that it loses confidence in the Lord and the authority He has given the believer and the Church. If one doesn't believe in the existence of an enemy, there will be no warfare. If one believes the enemy to be too powerful to fight, there will also be no warfare—only the passion to escape such a terrifying opponent.

Another characteristic of "Dunkirk" thinking in our churches is the losing sight of the Church's own authority and power. One of the marks proving Peter and John had been with Jesus was their confidence and boldness as they preached in the temple after the Lord's Resurrection.[7] The "Dunkirk" church is marked by its timidity and distaste for spiritual warfare. It forgets that Jesus has given His Church the keys to the Kingdom of God, the authority to use the resources of the Kingdom.

A limited view of spiritual warfare is another aspect of "Dunkirk" thinking. The war is waged "out there" somewhere. In truth, the war of the cosmos is a battle between the Third Heaven (God's realm) and the second heaven (satan's realm) for the destiny of the first heaven (the created realm). But the first heaven is the theater of war. Thus, if the Church longs to be taken from the world, she is like an army who doesn't understand it has been

7. Acts 4:13.

placed in the field of battle, not to be withdrawn, but to win the war.

Perhaps the greatest cause of the "Dunkirk" mindset is the escapist eschatology that developed in the Church. Every facet of God's cosmic plan is a certainty, and it is definite and beyond question that Jesus Christ will return to the earth in the Second Coming. His return is to be greatly anticipated and prepared for. Among other things, when Jesus comes back, He will establish His Kingdom fully and completely in the earth.

However, escapist eschatology is more focused on the Church's departure from the world than on the complete establishment of the Kingdom at the Second Coming. Rather than rejoicing over the coming victory of the Kingdom, escapists rejoice over the coming departure of the Church from the world. This results in an alienation from the Church's mission of battle and conquest.

Escapist eschatology revolves around the tremors over the Tribulation. No one wants to pass through the bitter trials of tribulation. So, it's understandable that excitement mounts as people anticipate being taken out of harm's way. Since escapist eschatology is so concerned with tribulation, it's important to consider what the Spirit says about it. Jesus mentions "great tribulation" in the Olivet Discourse:

> *Therefore when you see the abomination of desolation which was spoken of through Daniel the prophet, standing in the holy place (let the reader understand), then let those who are in Judea flee to the mountains; let him who is on the housetop not go down to get the things out that are in*

> *his house; and let him who is in the field not turn back to get his cloak. But woe to those who are with child and to those who nurse babes in those days! But pray that your flight may not be in the winter, or on a Sabbath; for then there will be a great tribulation, such as has not occurred since the beginning of the world until now, nor ever shall. And unless those days had been cut short, no life would have been saved; but for the sake of the elect those days shall be cut short* (Matthew 24:15-22).

"Tribulation" is from the Greek word, *thlipsis*, meaning "pressure." The picture is that of the massive stone that crushed juice from grapes and oil from olives. Jesus reveals that the triggering event for this great "pressure" that would fall on His people, is the "abomination of desolation," foreseen by Daniel.[8] The termination point of the "great tribulation," says Jesus, is determined by the "elect."

The historic events described in Daniel 11 apparently refer to Antiochus Epiphanes, a non-Jew who ruled Palestine almost 200 years prior to Christ's birth. He was committed to "hellenizing" the Jews, forcing Greek culture on them. His ultimate evil deed was sacrificing a pig on the high altar of the temple, cooking the meat, then spattering the building with the broth. This, the angel tells Daniel, is the "abomination" that causes desolation.

Whatever else the "abomination of desolation" may be, it is the offering up of reprehensible flesh in the place of spiritual sacrifice. The temple sacrifice was, again, a natural

8. Daniel 11:14-31.

type fulfilled ultimately in the cross of Jesus Christ. Jesus died because the world could not save itself. So, in the deepest sense, the "abomination of desolation" is man's attempt to put his own flesh on the cross. It is man trying to offer up reprehensible, fallen, corrupted human flesh to save reprehensible, fallen, corrupted human flesh.

The "abomination of desolation" is the whole miserable mess man has wrought in trying to place himself on the altar and be his own savior. It results in the horrific tribulation the human race brings on itself, including the suffering, oppression, persecution, wars, crime, sexual perversion, abortion on demand, drug abuse, terrorism, and vast catalogues of other miseries.

This is not to say there might not be a literal period when all the "little" tribulations mount up in one catastrophic tsunami of horror. But what escapist eschatology misses is the fact that history is merely the outward type of the deeper reality. Focusing so significantly on seven years of suffering that the spiritual issue is missed results in a "Dunkirk" mentality.

The "Normandy" Mentality in the Church

In contrast, the Normandy-minded church understands that, though there might be a Tribulation, the issue is not escape, but the fact that *it has authority to do something about it.* Only the Church Jesus builds can do anything substantive about the tribulation humanity brings upon itself. This is what He means when He says, in Matthew 24:22, that the period of "great tribulation" would be cut short "for the sake of the elect."

Many interpreters take this to mean that the great tribulation will be cut off because of its threat to the elect. This is not the meaning of the Greek terms used in the text. The word translated "for the sake of (the elect)" is *dia*. Literally, the term should be translated, "by means of." So, it is not "for the sake" of rescuing the saints from the dangers and miseries of the great tribulation, but it is "by means of" the "elect" that the great tribulation is cut short. The "elect" comprise the Church that Jesus builds, the one against whom the gates of hades won't prevail. Her intercessions and other works of authority are the means by which tribulation is cut off!

Thus, far from having an escapist eschatology, the "Normandy" church has a sense of vision, purpose, and a grasp of its authority to remain in the world and be the instrument God uses to cut off the tribulations man brings on himself by trying to be his own savior. It focuses its eschatology not on tribulation, but on the victory of the Kingdom to be revealed at the Second Coming of Christ. Even if a cross of tribulation lies in its path, life awaits on the other side.

Although the "Normandy" mentality is characterized by confidence and boldness, it is not triumphalistic. This attitude holds that victories come easily and without pain. This was Hitler's problem; he refused again and again to count the cost of war and to admit when his forces were beaten. Toward the end of the war, Allied armies were closing in on Hitler from all directions. Yet, as Winston Churchill notes, all this "had convinced all but Hitler and his closest followers that surrender was imminent and unavoidable."[9]

"Normandy"-minded people know differently. Private John Fitzgerald came into Ste. Mere-Eglise and saw dead paratroopers hanging from the trees. "They looked like rag dolls shot full of holes," he remembers. *"Their blood was dripping on this place they came to free."*[10] The "Normandy" church understands that the price of liberty for the universe is the blood of its Lord. And, since the Church is not greater than her Master, she knows that she, too, will suffer persecution while winning the victory.[11] So the Master hangs from a tree, His Blood dripping on the place He came to set free.

This doesn't mean the "Normandy" church succumbs to a victim mentality. Refusing triumphalism, the "Normandy" church counts the cost, suffers the counterattacks of the enemy, and yet sees itself as marching toward the inevitable moment of total conquest. As long as a church has the idea that it is a victim in the "devil's world," it will not be an effective combatant. Instead, it must see itself as one who will suffer, but who has come to take back God's world from the usurper. It must see itself as participating in a blessed invasion.

Svetlana, a young Serbian woman I know from Croatia, is a living example of the "Normandy" mentality. Driven

9. Winston Churchill, *Memoirs of the Second World War* (Boston: Houghton Mifflin Company, 1987), 941.
10. Stephen E. Ambrose, *D-Day, June 6, 1944: The Climatic Battle of World War II* (New York: Simon and Schuster, 1994), 274.
11. John 15:20.

from her home to Belgrade, Svetlana's vision is to return to Croatia to minister to those who forced her into exile.

Vassily, an engineer and disciple of Jesus Christ I met in a former communist nation, is another. The Lord told him to go and live in a certain town, even though there were no other believers there. Nevertheless, he sensed the Lord wanted him to "occupy" the town. For years, he lived there as the only follower of Christ. Finally, after 15 years, there were 30 believers. A catalytic process began through the "occupation" of Vassily, and he is confident there will be many more disciples in the future.

What inspires believers like Svetlana and Vassily to stand firm in enemy territory? What is the key to the "Normandy" mentality in the church? The answer is "Kingdom vision."

Kingdom Vision in the Church

If a church is to exhibit the attitudes of advancement and conquest, it must view the struggle from the perspective of the Kingdom of God. There are several "tests" that reveal whether or not Kingdom vision is present.

The first of these is the question: "*How far can you see?*" This was the issue Jesus posed to Simon Peter at Caesarea Philippi:

> *From that time Jesus Christ began to show His disciples that He must go to Jerusalem, and suffer many things from the elders and chief priests and scribes, and be killed, and be raised up on the third day. And Peter took Him aside and began to rebuke Him, saying, "God forbid it,*

> *Lord! This shall never happen to You." But He turned and said to Peter, "Get behind Me, Satan! You are a stumbling block to Me; for you are not setting your mind on God's interests, but man's." Then Jesus said to His disciples, "If anyone wishes to come after Me, let him deny himself, and take up his cross, and follow Me* (Matthew 16:21-24).

Peter's vision was earth-bound, limited to the short-term and immediate. Jesus had Kingdom vision, which looked beyond earthly limits all the way to the grand vista of the Kingdom's full victory. So, "for the joy set before Him [Jesus] endured the cross, despising the shame, and has sat down at the right hand of the throne of God."[12]

At every level, then, the Church must have Kingdom vision. The global Church must see herself advancing in the world rather then being beaten back. Local churches must get their eyes above their immediate conflicts and trials and see their destiny. Individual followers of Christ must grasp the fact that everything that happens to them after they have submitted to the Lordship of Jesus Christ will be used of the Father to mold them into Christlikeness.

A second test for Kingdom vision is: "*How wide can you see?*" In John 4:35b, Jesus tells His disciples about the closeness of the harvest. "Lift up your eyes," He says, "and look on the fields, that they are white for harvest." Thus, Kingdom vision sees beyond local issues and limitations. It understands that the local is part of something much greater.

12. Hebrews 12:2b.

A church with Kingdom vision understands that it is not an empire unto itself, but part of the Church of Jesus Christ in her city, nation, and world. Rather than drawing back, it will engage in dynamic relationships with other parts of the Body, in which the church both gives of itself and draws strength from the other parts.

Kingdom vision is wide enough to see the expanse of the "fields." A church with Kingdom vision sees beyond one racial or economic group to the totality of the people and needs comprising its "fields." It will not limit itself to one neighborhood, but it will set out to touch a city. This draws a church into partnership with other parts of the Body in the same city.

Kingdom vision also sees the readiness of the harvest. "The fields are white unto harvest," says Jesus, who sees them as they really are. A church without Kingdom vision sees the immensity of the world's darkness and assumes that the world will be resistant to the gospel. Jesus sees it differently. To one with Kingdom vision, darkness is an *opportunity* not an obstacle. Kingdom vision knows that the deeper the moral darkness, the greater the hunger for purity and holiness; the more dismal the racial and ethnic darkness, the more the desire for the fellowship of the saints; the gloomier the economic darkness, the greater the yearning for Kingdom principles of money and stewardship.

A third test for Kingdom vision is: "*How narrow can you see?*" As Joshua took on the leadership of Israel at the Jordan River, God told him to look neither to the right nor to the left.[13] This is the issue of focus. Although Kingdom vision is far and wide, it is also precise and focused. This means that the church with Kingdom vision is not distracted. It moves on its vision for the whole, as well as its vision for its part in the whole. This will depend on its place in space and time and its mix of spiritual gifts.

Israel stood at the threshold of the Promised Land. Ten spies had been sent to scout out the land. They reported back on a country full of "milk and honey."[14] But there was a problem: The people were strong, the cities walled, and giants dwelled there.

Two of the spies, however, Joshua and Caleb, had Kingdom vision. They acknowledged that the task would be formidable but had a sense of God's destiny. They saw beyond that present moment. Caleb said, "We should by all means go up and take possession of it, for we shall surely overcome it."[15]

Sadly, the rest of the nation lacked Kingdom vision. They cried all night. They shrieked at God and Moses. Joshua, driven by his intense vision, beseeched them:

> *If the Lord is pleased with us, then He will bring us into this land, and give it to us—a land which flows with milk and honey. Only do not rebel against the Lord; and do not fear the people of the land, for they shall be our prey. Their protection has been removed from them, and the Lord is with us; do not fear them* (Numbers 14:8-9).

---

13. Joshua 1:7.
14. Numbers 13:27.
15. Numbers 13:30.

This is the essence of Kingdom vision, trusting in God's victory despite all appearances to the contrary. The church with Kingdom vision will not be distracted by friend or foe, but it will press on with a sharp and single-minded focus, confident of the Lord's victory.

In June, 1940, Churchill addressed Parliament, telling his people, and the world:

> "We shall fight on the beaches, we shall fight on the landing grounds, we shall fight in the fields and in the streets, we shall fight in the hills; we shall never surrender; and even if, which I do not for a moment believe, this island or a large part of it be subjugated and starving, then our Empire beyond the seas, armed and guarded by the British Fleet, would carry on the struggle, until, in God's good time, the New World, with all its power and might, steps forth to the rescue and liberation of the Old."

This is exactly what has happened in Jesus Christ. The eternal new world of the Kingdom of God stepped into time and space, coming to the rescue of the "old world" trapped in sin and oppression. Jesus will fight on through His Church. The battle that unfolds across space and time will have moments of crisis and terror as the enemy resists, but the armies of the Kingdom will not stop until the "old world" knows liberation.

Meanwhile, there is an enemy who wants to fill the earth with his evil character. He aims at nothing less than mastery of the world. Like Hitler in World War II, this demonic ruler will not relent until someone with the power to drive him back stands against him. A closer look at the enemy and his occupation will reveal why the Church today must be a "Normandy" church.

Chapter 2

The Eagle Over the Globe

On an autumn day in 1934, Adolf Hitler and his architect, Albert Speer got into a blue Mercedes and set out for the Bavarian city of Nuremberg. Crossing through the Thuringian forest, they entered a village where, too late to organize a reception, the townspeople recognized them. Hitler told his companions it would be different at the next town. Nazi party hacks would call ahead. As He predicted, they were met there by adoring throngs of people.

Why Nuremburg?

Hitler had great plans for the city—a party rally site greater than the palace of the Persian kings at Persepolis, with a statue 46 feet taller than the Statue of Liberty, and a 400,000 seat stadium twice the size of ancient Rome's Circus Maximus. The entire complex would encompass a volume three times that of Cheop's pyramid. Looming over it all would be the two all-pervasive symbols of Hitler's regime, a swastika clasped in the talons of a huge eagle.

Hitler was obsessed with architectural mega-monuments. His most extreme plan was the one he envisioned for Berlin in 1939, a massive hall capped by a mountainous dome rising 957 feet above the streets. A globe would rest atop the dome and, as Hitler told Speer, "to crown this greatest building in the world, the eagle must stand above the globe."

Why an eagle?

Every aspiring leader needs an emblem, something to represent his regime and to provide a rallying point for his followers. Hitler's choice of the eagle for his emblem is not surprising. The eagle has for many centuries and in many cultures symbolized power, or war, or conquest. Often, the eagle is drawn carrying victims, symbolizing the sacrifice of lower and inferior beings and the victory of higher powers.

What was in Hitler's mind as he chose the eagle as his symbol? What motivation lay behind his obsession with architectural mega-monuments? These grand schemes reveal a mind set on nothing less than global domination. Even though the United States and most of Europe failed or refused to recognize this until almost too late, Hitler's intentions were clear early on, at least to some of his closest confidants. Speer, writing decades later, recorded that the monuments were "an assertion of his claim to *world dominion.*"[1]

Josef Goebbels, Hitler's propaganda minister, also understood his Fuehrer's designs. On May 8, 1943, Goebbels scribbled in his diary:

1. Albert Speer, *Inside the Third Reich* (New York: The Macmillan Company, 1970), 82, emphasis added.

"The Fuehrer expresses his unshakeable conviction that the Reich will one day rule all of Europe... And from then on the road to world domination is practically spread out before us. For whoever rules Europe will be able to seize the leadership of the world."[2]

Hitler knew he would not live forever, so, like countless other tyrants and emperors before him, he sought to leave great monuments and structures that would endure for centuries as testimonies to his glory.

What kind of man sets his mind on world domination?

German historian Friedrich Meinecke believed Hitler to be "one of the great examples of the singular and incalculable power of a personality in historical life—in this case *a plainly demonic personality*."[3]

Paul Schmidt, Hitler's prime translator, remembered the day Hitler made a triumphal procession through Nuremberg. Delirium gripped the adoring crowds. Schmidt wrote, "I was again impressed with the facial expression of an almost *biblical devotion* with which these people looked at Hitler as if in ecstasy and almost bewitched."[4]

There were numerous psychological profiles of Hitler. Henry A. Murray wrote that the Nazi leader displayed

2. Louis P. Lochner, ed., *The Goebbels Diaries* (New York: Doubleday, 1948), 359.
3. Horst Von Malitz, *The Evolution of Hitler's Germany* (New York: McGraw-Hill, 1973), 318, emphasis added.
4. Malitz, *Evolution*, 321, emphasis added.

"classical symptoms of paranoid schizophrenia," including "delusions of omnipotence and messiahship." Erikson saw Hitler as "an amoral sadistic infant." Edward Deuss, after 18 months of contact with Hitler, termed the Fuhrer "a man on the borderline of woman," and Ernst Hanfstaengl thought Hitler to be "both homosexual and heterosexual." Erik Fromm found Hitler to be "an almost totally necrophilous, narcissistic and incestuous person." That is, he loved death, worshipped himself, and reserved sexual relationship for those closest to him. Further, said Fromm, a "necrophilous person is attracted to darkness and night," which was apparent in Hitler's preference for a late-night lifestyle.[5] In short, Hitler was the embodiment and summation of the worst of human traits.

What philosophical beliefs drove such a man?

There were several key factors in the development of Nazi philosophy. One was a general decline of Biblical authority and religious traditions in the West, and particularly in Germany. The Age of Reason and the Enlightenment of the eighteenth and nineteenth centuries gave rise to the rationalist-based school of higher criticism that subjected the Bible to the same critical scrutiny given to other works of literature. Among other things, higher criticism attacked the Mosaic authorship of the first five books of the Bible, challenged the genealogy of Noah's descendents, and generally denied the Bible's supernatural claims.

The decline of traditional Judeo-Christian thought in Europe opened the door for Eastern philosophy to flow in

5. All above references from Malitz, *Evolution*, 317ff.

and fill the void. Johann-Gottfried Herder, a German Lutheran pastor and one of the founders of higher criticism, denied the biblical genealogy of Noah's descendents that made all people "half-brothers of the jews" (*sic.*). Rather, he traced Germanic origins to the Persians and, morally, to the Indians. One result of this influx of Eastern thought was the rise of the myth of Aryanism, or the purity of races, which held up the Germanic peoples as the purest and highest race, superior to all others.

The philosophical root of Aryanism lies in Eastern Hinduism and, in particular, the concept of brahmanism. The caste system in India derives from the Hindu worldview based on "Purusha," the "cosmic person." The Brahman caste is the highest and purest race, and it represents the "head" of Purusha. The other castes follow: Kshatriya ("shoulders"), Vaishya ("abdomen"), and Shudra ("feet"). In the ancient Aryan society of the Indus valley, this translated to warrior-nobles, priests, workmen, and serfs.

These ideas struck a responsive chord with European racialists. In 1804, August-Wilhelm Schlegel wrote that "Germany must be considered the Orient of Europe." Arthur Schopenhauer, who developed the most important pro-Aryan and antisemitic philosophical system in terms of its impact on the thought that would become nazism, wrote in *The World as Will and Idea*:

> "In India, our religions will never take root. The ancient wisdom of the human race will not be displaced by what happened in Galilee. On the contrary, Indian philosophy streams back to

Europe, and will produce a fundamental change in our knowledge and thought."[6]

Arthur de Gobineau, a Frenchman, believed race was the determinant in the rise and fall of civilizations. The Semites had polluted the pure Aryan stock—now embraced by important German philosophers as their forebears—and it was up to the Teutons, or Germans, to restore racial purity. Intellectually and spiritually, then, we see that many Europeans—not only Germans—were prepared to accept the theories of the Nazis.

It is not surprising, then, that many people who witnessed the horrors of the Third Reich wondered if Hitler was the antichrist. Although it is now clear that Hitler was not *the* Antichrist prophesied in Revelation, there can be little doubt that he was an *expression* of antichrist. The biblical concept of "antichrist" refers not only to an individual person or persons, but also to a demonic spirit that has been in the world from the beginning.[7]

The Greek *antichristos* means "against Christ," or "instead of Christ." Westcott combines the two ideas, and renders the term, "one who, assuming the guise of Christ, opposes Christ." Antichrist, then, describes any person, regime, philosophy, or movement that seeks to oppose or supplant Christ. This antichrist spirit has made itself known throughout human history, pervading all mankind's attitudes, institutions, governments, and social structures. It has

6. Arthur Schopenhauer, *The World as Will and Idea* (place: publisher, date), page.
7. 1 John 4:3.

been particularly manifest whenever anyone has attempted to stand in the place of Christ as a human "messiah" or "savior" to the world.

Hitler, for example, said in a speech on March 20, 1936,

> "From the people I have come, within the people I have remained, to the people I shall return...I have taught you to have faith, now you shall give me your faith."

Hermann Goring, among others, was willing to place his faith in Hitler, as revealed in Malitz, *The Evolution of Hitler's Germany*. "God gave the savior to the German people," Goring said. "We have faith, deep and unshakable faith, that he was sent to us by God to save Germany." Goring was intoxicated by the spirit of antichrist.

There is only one pre-existent, omnipotent, omniscient, and omnipresent Spirit—the Most High God. All other spirits are created beings and, hence, finite. A spirit must find a physical creature to inhabit if it is to express itself in the realm of time and space.

The powers of darkness search primarily for people to inhabit and control. God's original design was to indwell His creation through His people, the human beings He created. Demons are usurpers, seeking to occupy that which is reserved for God. Since they are non-material spirits, they can only express themselves in the material world by inhabiting people. This is how the spirit of antichrist has worked through many people across history. Thus, writes John, "many antichrists have arisen."[8]

---

8. 1 John 2:18.

This same spirit motivated the writers of *Humanist Manifesto II* to declare that "no god [*sic.*] can save us...we must save ourselves." It is this spirit that compels many politicians to position themselves as the saviors of the electorate and to preach subtle lies in 30-second chunks of television. It is this spirit that drives technocrats to declare that education, science, and technology will save humanity. It was the spirit of antichrist that energized Marx and Engels and Lenin to believe that they could build a new paradise through communism.

The antichrist spirit has several general characteristics. First, it denies the deity of Jesus Christ.[9] It refuses to ascribe transcendence to Christ, and it seeks to reduce Him to the lowest level. This is graphically illustrated in the increasing usage of Christ's name as a swear word. In the American entertainment media there appears to be a conscious effort to find opportunities to so use His name. Why aren't the names of Mohammed or Buddha used in such a fashion? Those names are not offensive to the spirit of antichrist.

The spirit of antichrist also denies that Christ has come in the flesh.[10] If the rejection of Christ's deity is the denial of His transcendence, then the disbelief in His incarnation is the denial of His immanence.

Another characteristic of the antichrist spirit is the attempt to dethrone Christ from His rightful place as Lord

9. 1 John 2:22.
10. 2 John 7.

and to hold up in His stead some human philosophy, thought, idea, or institution as the savior of humanity. This is the essence of humanism, that man save himself by his own wisdom and efforts.

How did this spirit of antichrist enter the physical, created realm in the first place? If everything that God created was "good,"[11] then where did such a sinister influence come from?

Prior to creation, the only realm was God's realm. The only sphere of authority was the throne of God. At some point before the physical universe came into existence, God created the lesser beings of the spirit world, the angels. Lucifer, one of the brightest and most beautiful of these, led a rebellion in Heaven, seeking to overthrow God and assume for himself the place of "lord." His failure and subsequent expulsion from Heaven brought about the emergence of a second, inferior sphere of authority temporarily established under his rule. At the moment of creation of the physical universe, another sphere of authority appeared, that of human beings.

The Greek word for heaven, *ouranos*, conveys the idea of elevation. It suggests not only the sky, or the final destiny of God's people, but also a *dominion*. The highest Heaven, or dominion, where God abides on His throne, is the "Third Heaven."[12] The second heaven is the one temporarily under lucifer's control. The first heaven is the created

11. Genesis 1.
12. 2 Corinthians 12:2.

physical realm originally under the dominion of human beings.

God's Kingdom in eternity is characterized by order, peace, unity, harmony, and love—all held together by His benevolent authority. His original design in creation was to impart the same order in that sphere of authority placed under the stewardship of humans, whom God created in His own image.

Lucifer's rebellion introduced chaos into the orderly "cosmos" of God's Kingdom. He attacked the very throne of God, the source and symbol of all authority. Without that authority, all is disorder. Lucifer's attack, then, struck at the very foundation of the order that insures that reality is cosmos and not chaos.

This assault on God's throne is recorded in Isaiah 14:12-17:

> *How you have fallen from heaven, O star of the morning, son of the dawn! You have been cut down to the earth, you who have weakened the nations! But you said in your heart, "I will ascend to heaven; I will raise my throne above the stars of God, and I will sit on the mount of the assembly in the recesses of the north. I will ascend above the heights of the clouds; I will make myself like the Most High." Nevertheless you will be thrust down to Sheol, to the recesses of the pit. Those who see you will gaze at you, they will ponder over you, saying, "Is this the man who made the earth tremble, who shook kingdoms, who made the world like a wilderness and overthrew its cities, who did not allow his prisoners to go home?*

As matter and anti-matter cannot co-exist, neither can cosmos and chaos. Lucifer and his legions were hurled from Heaven. As he descended, *lucifer*, whose name means "brightness," became *satan*, whose name means "opponent" or "adversary." Since his fall, satan has exercised corrupt authority in a spiritual domain between God's Heaven and the physical realm. He imposes this authority on the earth, the "capital" of the created order, where mankind dwells. All authority, of course, comes from God. Even satan's authority is an illicit and perverse use of God's authority. God allows this for a time because He created reality to operate with freedom. Freedom to choose is essential to freedom to love. God desires the love of men, but He does not force it. It must be by free choice. In the context of that freedom, satan is able to pervert authority.

God's original intent was to rule over the entire universe, with man as His regent ruling over natural creation, the "first heaven." Lucifer's fall brought about the "second heaven," from which he seeks to impose his rule over the first heaven. Jesus Christ came to earth as the bearer of God's Kingdom rule, bringing it back into the created domain. The Church, as the Body of Christ, is the organism through which the Holy Spirit continues the Kingdom ministry of Jesus. Thus, *the Church is the army of the Third Heaven, living in the first heaven, battling the second heaven for the destiny of the first heaven.*

Satan's goal in invading the earth with the spirit of antichrist is clear. It's not only the earth he wants, but also the whole of the universe. He is still reaching for the Throne of creation, seeking to restore the glory he lost when he was cast out of Heaven. His desire is to thwart God's original purpose to fill the universe with His glory. Instead, satan wants creation at his feet. In short, he wants to be the lord of creation.

"Children, it is the last hour," says John, "and just as you know that antichrist is coming, even now many antichrists have arisen; from this we know that it is the last hour."[13] Because of the lateness of the hour, the spirit of antichrist will intensify in the world. The term, "last," means the "utmost" or "the extreme" of time. "Hour," in Greek, refers not only to a moment, but also to a season. In this sense, the "last hour" began with Pentecost, the dawning of the era of the Church, or the "age of the Gentiles." This is that period foreseen by Jesus when the Gentiles would be the primary ministers of the Kingdom rather than Israel.[14]

In the meantime, satan works tirelessly to fill the earth with his evil character. One of his key strategies is to draw the people and nations of the world toward a single world order, one global system under his evil power, with no boundaries or refuge from it. This is what Hitler tried to do. There are many trends at the end of the twentieth century that are driving the world toward satan's goal of one global order. World empire is the goal of the antichrist spirit, and with it, the global reign of antichrist's master, satan himself.

13. 1 John 2:18.
14. See Matthew 21:43; Luke 21:24.

Chapter 3

Globalism: Into the Arms of Antichrist

As the world approaches the twenty-first century, it appears to be moving closer and closer to satan's goal of global dominion. The modern "Normandy"-minded church needs to move through these times with its eyes wide open and its heart secure in its faith in Christ, in the authority He has given His Church to work in the world, and in the certainty of His victory in the end. An understanding of the "seasons" of the "last hour," which has been in place since Pentecost, as mentioned in the previous chapter, will help the Church today know what to expect and how to respond.

Since the time of the first century Church, the history of man has passed through several "seasons" that have involved changes of his perspective and outlook toward himself, his world, and spiritual things, particularly the transcendence and immanence of God.

During the Middle Ages, the primary focus was on God's transcendence. He was high and lofty, mysterious, and austere. This is seen clearly in the architecture of the great medieval cathedrals. They are marvels of design and execution, soaring to awesome heights and symbolizing the mystery and "otherness" of God.

The Renaissance of the fourteenth and fifteenth centuries began with the rediscovery of the classic societies of ancient Greece and Rome. The Greeks worshipped nature, including man as its highest expression. The Romans deified the emperor and the state system. The Greeks patterned their gods after flawed mortals, which lowered them to man's level, while the Romans exalted man and a human system of government to the level of gods. The result was a diminished regard for the transcendent character of deity. Renaissance thought embraced many of these philosophies, and men began to lose sight of God's transcendence.

The season of "Enlightenment" followed the Renaissance. This was the Age of Reason, when man's rational capacities ruled, and all the supernatural and superstitious mysteries of the world were to fall before the logic and reason of men. Its defining moment came one day during the eighteenth century when Frenchmen hoisted a street woman on their shoulders, carried her into the cathedral of Notre Dame, and proclaimed her the symbol of the "Goddess of Reason."

The progression of seasons continued, giving rise in the twentieth century to the Age of Utilitarianism. Human life became defined by its quality, not its intrinsic value. The implications of this are ominous. Abortion, euthanasia, and assisted suicide are some of the results. Utilitarianism is humanism at its extreme: If the human being is transcendent (that is, highest), then the human being has the right to define what qualifies as human and who has the right to live.

According to science, at one time aeons ago all the land mass of the earth was gathered together in one place. Due to the shifting of tectonic plates, this land mass broke into pieces, which slowly drifted over the centuries—bumping into each other, pushing up mountains and forming valleys—until they reached their present geographical locations. Whether or not this theory is true, it is a stark illustration of the reality of drifting nations.

In the earliest days of humanity there was oneness. This was true in Eden, and it was true for quite a while after the fall. There was no ethnnic plurality. There were no boundaries *between people*; there was only the boundary that separated Eden from what was beyond Eden. The fall into sin was a cataclysm that divided people and set everything adrift. Humanity was cut off from its Anchor, the God of the universe.

God's plan was for man to multiply, spread over the face of the earth, and subdue it. Man had other ideas. Even as the human race proliferated, it stayed together, with a single language and culture. Man was determined to go his own way.

At the heart of this determination was the urge to be God. This desire for self-deification still burns in man's heart. Man would ignore God's command and build a tower as the center of his civilization. It would exert a magnetic pull on humanity, welding the race together.

God is absolute and so are His decrees. Language was confounded at Babel, and the people were scattered over the face of the earth. They began to drift. God established boundaries, lest the collision of the peoples destroy the planet.

> *And He has made from one blood every nation of men to dwell on all the face of the earth, and has determined their preappointed times and the boundaries of their dwellings* (Acts 17:26 NKJ).

Why boundaries?

Boundaries are unnecessary in a world without sin. In a fallen world, however, they are essential. They protect against anarchy and against the collisions of nation against nation. Boundaries separate contentious children and come between animals that instinctively hate one another. God's design was for no national or ethnic divisions between people. Since that did not happen, God revealed how fallen man may maintain order in a world abandoned to chaos. Borders and boundaries are part of that revelation. God has fixed boundaries to restrain sin for humanity's good.

The goal of antichrist is to establish a one-world order in which there are no boundaries. Without boundaries there is no concept of the sacred. Antichrist desires the borderless world because he wants to obliterate the notion of the sacred. Boundaries in a fallen world create problems, but a world without them is an even greater peril.

Hitler, driven by the spirit of antichrist, believed "the concept of the 'nation' has become empty."[1] He wanted to do away with the global arrangement of nations and reconfigure the world according to race. This, he said, would result in a "rearranging of boundaries."[2]

Harvard Professor Samuel P. Huntington, writing in the Summer, 1993, issue of *Foreign Affairs*, has this intriguing observation:

> "World politics is entering a new phase...the principle conflicts of global politics will occur between nations and groups of different civilizations. The clash of civilizations will dominate global politics. The fault lines between civilizations will be the battle lines of the future."

The proponents of the "global village," where boundaries are removed, claim it would promote peace and understanding among people. This is a naive view because it ignores the reason God gave boundaries in the first place. Man is a violent, bloodthirsty sinner, living in a tooth and claw world. One group must be walled off from other groups wishing to destroy it. John Dawson, understanding the importance of boundaries, writes,

> "In mercy, God has appointed nations to restrain the course of humankind's self-destructive potential.

1. Malitz, *Evolution*, 233.
2. Malitz, *Evolution*, 233.

> Imagine if the world were united under one central government and the system became utterly corrupted. There would be no nations of refuge to run to...no independent states that could form righteous alliance against tyranny."[3]

Jesus knew that colliding civilizations would precede His coming. Matthew 24:7 records, "For nation will rise against nation, and kingdom against kingdom...." Civilizations collide as nations drift aimlessly in an anchorless world. Cultural differences and opposing value systems create misunderstanding and hostility between civilizations.

The "anchor" of a civilization is its value system. Every civilization has a value system, or code of social, moral, and religious beliefs. Anchorless nations are those who do not base their value system on God and His Kingdom.

Some argue that the culture of the West is absolute. V.S. Naipaul says that "Western civilization is the 'universal civilization' that 'fits all men.' " This only converts Western civilization into an idol. The "universal civilization" is the Kingdom of God. As long as men look to earthly kingdoms for that role, the differences will only deepen, and the clashes intensify.

There are three particular trends evident in this drift of the nations. The first of these is human-based materialism, or the idea that the production, distribution, and consumption of material things to satisfy the needs of man constitute absolute value. Communist nations drifted in

3. John Dawson, *Healing America's Wounds* (Ventura: Regal Books), 126.

the direction of dialectical materialism while capi
tions moved toward practical materialism. It is ironic that Marxist Communism and Western capitalism are two different expressions of the same human-based materialism.

The second trend is toward a counterfeit spirituality. There is a genuine spiritual life, energized by the Spirit of God and vitalizing the human spirit. It makes human beings "partakers of the divine nature,"[4] and produces in them the spiritual fruit of love, joy, peace, patience, kindness, goodness, faithfulness, gentleness and self-control.[5]

Counterfeit spirituality, on the other hand, is a "form of godliness," which denies the power of true spiritual life.[6] It is "dead works," man attempting to merit the favor of God in his own power.[7] It is dependence on man-made traditions rather than God's Word.[8] Counterfeit spirituality attempts to do in man's power what only God can do.

Counterfeit spirituality usually contains elements of either the cult or the occult, sometimes both. The cult centers around one powerful individual, personality, or idea that becomes almost divine in the minds of followers. Hitler was a cultic figure to many. The occult focuses on a compact with satanic and demonic supernatural forces through astrology, magic, witchcraft and other practices. Again, Hitler had an obsessive interest in the occult. Either

4. 2 Peter 1:4.
5. Galatians 5:22-23.
6. 2 Timothy 3:5.
7. Hebrews 6:1-2.
8. Mark 7:13.

way, cult or occult, the source of counterfeit spirituality is the same—satan.

Eventually the broad tributaries of humanist materialism and counterfeit spirituality converge, forming one immense river: human-based religion. This is becoming especially evident in the United States and other Western societies. It is religious in its mystical characteristics and materialistic in its objective characteristics, relying on the material world and human flesh. It is counterfeit because it begins with man rather than God. Hence, it is a denial of the transcendence of God and an attempt to make man and nature transcendent.

By definition, created things cannot be transcendent, for this would infer that the creature is above the Creator. The result would be chaos. Yet this is precisely what all human-based systems try to do and why the nations are adrift. To paraphrase Dostoevsky, if there is no God, or if God is dead, then all things are permitted. The only way to believe in the transcendence of the created order is to deny the transcendent reality of the Creator. When this happens, then man, his civilizations, and his nations are all separated from their Anchor and drift aimlessly toward chaos and death.

One result of this drift is that war is the norm for civilization, rather than the exception. Sociologist Pitirim Sorokin discovered that Russia, over the last millennium, has been at war in 46 of every 100 years. England has fought with other nations for 56 of every 100 years since the era of William the Conqueror. Australian scholar

Geoffrey Blainey writes that an "obstacle to studying international peace is perhaps the widespread assumption that it is the normal state of affairs." Such a conclusion, he says, is "inaccurate."[9] The world experiences "outbreaks of peace," not "outbreaks of war."

A third result of the drift of nations is that as the world approaches the twenty-first century, nations have begun to disintegrate. Robert D. Kaplan, writing on "The Coming Anarchy," in *The Atlantic Monthly*, describes the chaos in several African states where bedlam reigns. "Such," he says, "is becoming *the* symbol of worldwide demographic, environmental and societal stress, in which criminal anarchy emerges as the real 'strategic' danger."[10] His article appeared just two months before the shocking bloodbath was unleashed in Rwanda, described by some reporters as setting a new standard of horror in the world. The world map of the future, Kaplan predicts, will "never be static." In a sense, it will be the "Last Map," and "will be an ever-mutating representation of chaos."

Physicists in the late twentieth century began to probe chaos in nature. Natural chaos is merely an outward manifestation of the root chaos underlying the created realm. It is this root chaos that lies behind the "groaning" and "travail" of the universe.[11] The Bible says that natural creation

9. Geoffrey Blainey, *The Causes of War* (New York: The Free Press, 1973).
10. Robert D. Kaplan, "The Coming Anarchy," *The Atlantic Monthly*, February, 1994, 44ff, emphasis added.
11. Romans 8:18-23.

has been "subjected to futility" and awaits its rescue. Therein lies the hope. "The creation itself also will be delivered from the bondage of corruption into the glorious liberty of the children of God."[12] Thus, the moaning of the created order is that of birth pangs, not despair.[13] Those who do not know or accept God's revelation of what is really happening do not discern the hope.

Chaos has sucked creation into a terrifying, powerful vortex. Everything is caught in the maelstrom. Put another way, this vortex might be called "spiritual gravity." The biblical worldview is that everything in nature is a witness to the supernatural reality that lies behind it. Romans 1:20 says, "For since the creation of the world His [God's] invisible attributes...have been clearly seen, being understood through what has been made...." In the words of Psalm 19:1, "The heavens are telling of the glory of God; and their expanse is declaring the work of His hands." Therefore, physical gravity in the natural realm witnesses to the deeper reality of spiritual gravity in the supernatural realm.

When Hitler and his armies invaded France, they forced their way into territory not their own. Hitler flaunted international law, ignored the sanctity of borders, and imposed his rule on France. Hitler reduced the cosmos of balance and harmony, which was to exist between nations and without which peace is impossible, to the chaos of invasion and occupation.

12. Romans 8:21 NKJ.
13. Romans 8:22.

In a much larger spiritual sense, the earth is also an occupied zone. Satan and his forces have seized temporary control of the planet. It is not their rightful rule. "The earth is the Lord's, and the fulness thereof."[14] It is sovereign territory, occupied by an evil oppressor. This is the worldview that must compel every follower of Christ.

As did Hitler in World War II, so the antichrist spirit seeks global empire. The current drive toward globalism is a dash into the arms of antichrist. Many world leaders advocate a one-world system which they believe will solve the planet's problems. Currently there are numerous moves in this direction. A look at a few of these trends will show the subtle but unmistakable drive toward a world without boundaries.

Boutros Boutros-Ghali and the United Nations

Although he is no longer Secretary General of the United Nations, Boutros Boutros-Ghali still expresses the philosophies that underly the global organization:

> "As the 21st century approaches, the planet is in the grip of two vast, opposing forces: globalization and fragmentation. Globalization is creating a world that is increasingly interconnected, in which national boundaries are less important, and is generating both possibilities and problems."[15]

14. Psalm 24:1a KJV.
15. Boutros Boutros-Ghali, "Global Leadership After the Cold War," *Foreign Affairs*, vol. 75, no. 2, March/April 1996, 86-98.

Although not advocating world government, Boutros-Ghali clearly believes the UN is the answer to these problems. "As if in training for precisely this moment, the United Nations has in its 50 years gained enormous experience in contending with the problems that both have spawned."[16] His solution to the problems of globalization, however, is more globalization: a UN-defined set of "human rights for the international community," a UN-advanced extension of international law, and a UN-promoted "consensus on disarmament, the environment, population, social development, migration, and the advancement of women."[17]

When he writes of "consensus," Boutros-Ghali mentions one of the most disturbing aspects of globalization. Many believe a human conspiracy lies behind the current emphasis on globalism. Although there *is* a conspiracy of spiritual powers behind world history, what propels the world toward globalism is a consensus of her elites—journalists, academics, religious leaders, and all others who shape public opinion. A consensus is much harder to fight than a conspiracy, because the enemy is less easy to identify. Consensus-building is intellectual and spiritual guerilla warfare. Boutros-Ghali's solution is to strengthen the UN: "As the international community works its way toward a consensus on these intellectual and moral questions, the secretary-general must take a central role in resolving the conflict between realism and

16. Boutros-Ghali, "Global Leadership," 87.
17. Boutros-Ghali, "Global Leadership," 87.

responsibility."[18] However, the UN's efforts in this direction pose not a blessing to mankind, but a dark threat.

The Commission on Global Governance

It should come as no surprise, then, that Boutros-Ghali blessed the formation of the Commission on Global Governance, designed by former German Chancellor Willy Brandt and chaired by Ingvar Carlsson of Sweden and Shridath Ramphal of Guyana. The Commission's report, *Our Global Neighborhood,*[19] states that a need exists "to weave a tighter fabric of international norms, expanding the rule of law worldwide and enabling citizens to exert their democratic influence on global processes," and that "the world's arrangements for the conduct of its affairs must be underpinned by certain common values." Law will not work nor organizations stand unless built on the foundation of "shared values."

An internationalist believes nations must interact and opposes isolationism. A Christian internationalist is sensitive to cultural differences, respects them, and seeks to work within their context. Although agreeing that desperate nations need aid, that alliances are sometimes necessary, and discussion between nations is a must, he understands that the well-being of the planet depends on the existence of borders within which local authority can function. This requires recognition of the sovereign nature of states. The

18. Boutros-Ghali, "Global Leadership," 94, emphasis added.
19. Commission on Global Governance, *Our Global Neighborhood* (Oxford University Press, 1995), xiv.

ordering of nations, therefore, is itself a deterrant to those seeking global tyranny.

In contrast, the worldview of contemporary globalists is based on a concept of man arising from the thoughts of Enlightenment-era philosopher Jean-Jacques Rousseau. This naive view holds that man is fundamentally good until ruined by society and environment. It has no place for sin or the corrupted, fallen nature of man.

Though not advocating a formal world government in the political sense, the Commission does call for global systems and rules guided by "basic human values" but without addressing the question of who will define and enforce them. Millions believe the right to life is the fundamental "basic human value." Will this be a shared value upon which the global system is based, or will it be the value of the People's Republic of China, which mandates abortion for any pregnancies that exceed the state-prescribed limit? Who decides?

There are several fundamental characteristics essential to globalism. One of these is collectivism, which is, in theory, the shared ownership of all things collectively by the masses, but in practice it is always the proprietorship of the state with control by the few. The Commission says there is "no alternative to working together and using collective power to create a better world," and that the UN "must continue to play a central role in global governance."

Despite the collapse a decade ago of Communism and its centrally managed economy and the fact that many nations still struggle to energize the private sector and throw off central control, the Commission has laid the foundation for a globally managed economy: The "effective and equitable management" of the world's resources and problems "calls for a systemic, long-term, global approach, guided by the principle of sustainable development, which has been the central lesson from the mounting ecological dangers of recent times."

There are several chilling ramifications to this. First, "equitable management" could mean controlled distribution of wealth and denial of the right to private property. Second, any "systemic" approach involves authoritarian bureaucracies, which, in a global context, would inevitably become global government. Finally, "sustainable development" must be defined. By whom?

A second fundamental characteristic of globalism is media control. According to the Commission, "civil society itself should try to provide a measure of global public service broadcasting not linked to commercial interests." Since "civil society" is government, the Commission calls for nothing less than a global broadcasting system controlled by the collective.

Another fundamental is a centrally defined code of morality and ethics. "Global values must be the cornerstone of global governance," says the Commission. The values of the past simply don't suit today's needs. Since God has no place in this global scheme, *someone* must define the moral code. But *who*? The Commission itself has proposed these parameters: The core values are respect for life (though there is no prohibition of abortion or euthanasia), "liberty, justice and equity, mutual respect, caring, and integrity." Economic exchange and the new global media will bind people together into a "universal moral community" with its "shared values."

Certainly the nations of the world should work together to solve mutual problems. A great danger exists, however, in building a global structure that focuses on the perfectibility of man and ignores the absolute authority and sovereignty of God.

It Takes A Village

The collectivist impulse is at the heart of Hillary Rodham Clinton's folksy, disarmingly sweet book, *It Takes A Village*. The title is taken from an African proverb that says children thrive only if their families thrive and if society as a whole cares enough to provide for them. A more honest title for Mrs. Clinton's book would be "*It Takes A Collective.*"

According to Mrs. Clinton, today's village is not a clustering of huts or "Hometown U.S.A., population 5,340," but the "network of values and relationships that support and affect our lives." Such a network, she suggests, is essential for raising today's children. The inference is that the values and beliefs of a particular family may be too narrow, intolerant, or restrictive.

Mrs. Clinton believes people "cannot move forward by looking to the past for easy solutions." Apparently, history is of little value to the new world order. "Instead," she says, "our challenge is to arrive at a consensus of values and common vision of what we can do today, individually and collectively, to build strong families and communities." Building consensus means "resisting the lure of extremist rhetoric." This statement reminds one of those described by Allan Bloom, who believe that "[t]here is no enemy other than the man who is not open to everything."[20] The extremist, then, is the "true believer." Who defines "extremist"?

In reality, it doesn't take a village to raise a child, but a family. The fact that children today are reared in the context of a global village doesn't mean they *should* be. A good example of the proper balance of this concept is the ancient, village-dwelling Jewish family. Although the children clearly grew up in the context of the village, each family had clear instructions from God on how to raise them. The father was the spiritual head of the family. Jewish parents were the educators, the conveyors of life-skills and the transmitters, not of a "consensus of values," but of the *absolute values* handed down by a holy, living God. It is precisely this type home, built around a father and mother, that today's family revisionists so despise. As long as such a home exists, the collective has a hard time imposing its control.

Mrs. Clinton also states that even spiritual renewal is the work of the collectivist village. In such a model, religious life in the village has no room for the " true believer" who proclaims that God or the gospel or the Torah or the Koran favors a particular political action, and that anyone who opposes him is "on the side of the devil." Such a person

20. Allan Bloom, *The Closing of the American Mind* (New York: Simon and Schuster, 1987), 27.

"is asserting an absolutist position that permits no compromise, no deference to the will of the majority, no acceptance of decisions by those in authority—all necessities for the function of any democracy." In such a society the only evil is "intolerance," the only enemy the "true believer."

Mrs. Clinton believes that the education of children is also the responsibility of the collective. Her views reflect the educational philosophy of John Dewey, considered by many to be the most influential American educator of the twentieth century. Dewey believed, first of all, that there are no eternal principles and thus no absolutes. Consequently, there are no true individuals, only organisms conditioned by the collective. Since the mind is formed by society, there is no individual mind. John Whitehead says that for Dewey, the human mind was "public property, an element of the collective."[21] For Dewey, then, it not only takes a village to raise a child, but the child is the *property* of the village.

How did Dewey arrive at his conclusions? According to J. Minor Gwynn, four motives have historically driven American education: the *religious* (1635-1770); the *political* (1770-1860); the *utilitarian* (1860-1920); and *mass education* (1920-present).[22] Dewey was a product of the utilitarian period, which considered the role of education to be not knowledge for its own sake, but to equip people for work.

21. John W. Whitehead, *The Stealing of America* (Westchester, Illinois: Crossway Books, 1983), 17.
22. J. Minor Gwynn, *Curriculum Principles and Social Trends* (New York: The Macmillan Co., 1960), 35.

Workers are vital to the collective. The next logical step was mass education, to ensure a continuous supply of workers for the collective.

Mrs. Clinton's collectivist village would be a comfortable home for B.F. Skinner, proponent of behavior modification and control and developer of the method known as operant conditioning. Isolated small tasks are reinforced until they merge into a behavior. Skinner believes that no one is a person at birth, but that each becomes a person upon acquiring a repertoire of behavior. He says that "there is no place in the scientific position for a self as a true originator or initiator of action."[23] According to Morris L. Bigge, Skinner's theory means that the real work of psychologists is to "gain more understanding of conditions under which reinforcement works best, thereby opening the way for cultural control through social engineering."[24]

Cultural control is at the heart of collectivism, which is at the heart of globalism. Hillary Rodham Clinton's *It Takes A Village* reinforces all three.

The Gorbachev Forum

Though apparently exiled to the fringes of Russian political life, Mikhail Gorbachev remained the darling of many Western opinion makers. In September, 1995, 250 of them paid $5,000 each to attend his "State of the World Forum" in San Francisco.

23. B.F. Skinner, *About Behaviorism* (New York: Alfred A. Knopf, 1974), 225.
24. Morris L. Bigge, *Learning Theories for Teachers*, Fourth Edition (New York: Harper and Row, 1982), 111.

The Forum launched a five-year plan to develop a world consensus on vision and priority for the twenty-first century. Its mission statement declares that "at this momentous juncture in history—between the ending of the Cold War and the dawn of the new century—we are experiencing the birth of the first global civilization." Jim Garrison, president of the Gorbachev Foundation, spoke of "the global civilization which lies ahead," and the "interdependence" at its various levels, "with each other...with the Earth...with the spirit which perennially guides the affairs of humankind."

That "spirit" is not a benign force leading the world to paradise, but an evil power seeking to substitute itself for the true King, and taking the world to chaos and doom.

The forum was underwritten by major corporations and reportedly attended by many "global citizens" such as Vice President Al Gore, former President George Bush, Jane Fonda, Deepak Chopra (a New Age leader), Bill Gates, Ted Koppel, Colin Powell, John Denver, Shirley MacLaine, Alvin Toffler, Carl Sagan, Margaret Thatcher and Ted Turner. It highlighted themes such as strengthening the UN, developing global values, and the need for collectivism, demonstrating the growing globalist consensus among the world's elites.

Gorbachev told the gathering that the world is in "a transition to a new civilization." A Global Brain Trust was needed to redraw boundaries politically, economically, socially, and spiritually. Echoing *Humanist Manifesto II*, astronomer Carl Sagan declared, "There is no hint that help will come from elsewhere to save ourselves." Roundtable discussions explored subjects such as global security, spirituality, and taxation. Joan M. Veon, reporting on the Forum for Intercessors for America, noted that "control and use of the Internet and indoctrination of the world's youth were seen to be pivotal in forming a new global civil society."[25]

Gorbachev himself sounded the key theme of the Forum when he called for a "new paradigm" that would "integrate all achievements of the human mind and human action, irrespective of which ideology or political movement can be credited with them." The search for this new paradigm would be a "search for synthesis...."

This synthesis would involve a global spirituality. Absolutist doctrines, such as Christianity, would be replaced by an inclusive value system set according to global human standards. Gorbachev believes the world suffers from a spiritual emptiness that the great leaders must find a way to fill. The new religious order must do away with the idea that one particular way is the only right one.

The Parliament of the World's Religions

There is evidence that this new world religion is already forming. In 1993, Chicago hosted the Parliament of the World's Religions, which claimed to have found the Holy Grail, the much-sought consensus of global ethics. The Parliament was determined to steer away from absolutist

25. Joan M. Veon, "Globalism: Gorbachev Convenes World Forum," *Intercessors for America Newsletter*, Nov. 1995, vol. 22, no. 11.

ideas like biblical Christianity. David Steindl-Rast, a Benedictine monk, refused to use Scriptures that mentioned Jesus, since that would spark disunity, or even any Scriptures that referred to God, since the idea of God was so masculine and sexist.

One of the speakers was Robert Muller, a New Ager and globalist who once served as Deputy General Secretary of the UN. He told the group that the only hope for saving the world from global pollution was the establishment of a global community. Facilitators from the MIT Dialogue Project took the delegates through steps helping them "let go" of one of their most cherished individual beliefs, if only for a moment. This was a practice session for the great global spirituality that would come about when the obstacles of cherished beliefs were dropped and the new global community envisioned by Muller and others was ushered in.

* * *

When the Germans invaded France, they used the tactic known as *blitzkrieg*, or, "lightning war." The term was coined by an American reporter to describe the fast and furious invasions of the Nazis. Developed in the 1930s and used by the Germans beginning in 1939, *blitzkrieg* began with a massive artillery and air bombardment of a weak place in the enemy's line. Then, armor would pour through the hole, with infantry following on a massive scale. It was total war.

When the devil invaded earth, he declared all-out war to crush everything belonging to the Kingdom of God. His artillery and air assaults come in the form of intense spiritual attacks. He constantly probes for weak points where he can hurl powerful force. Once a weak spot breaks, he sends in armies of demons to occupy and control. A weak spot in the world today is the current trend toward a global community without boundaries. Satan will exploit that weakness to its fullest extent. The "Normandy"-minded church must be alert to the destroyer's assault on these weak spots. Such points of attack must be discovered and strengthened. The people of God, residing in a zone of occupation, must understand that the only response to the enemy is the same—*all-out war*!

Chapter 4

The Boot of the Enemy

As Joshua prepared to lead Israel into Canaan, God promised him, "Every place on which the sole of your foot treads, I have given it to you, just as I spoke to Moses."[1] The "Nazi boot," as a symbol of widespread occupation, was a demonic parody of Joshua's "foot" of authority, just as the swastika was a perverted version of the cross. Through the centuries, the boot has symbolized enemy domination. To be "under the boot" is to be defeated and occupied.

Paris fell on June 15, 1940. Hitler's warriors thundered through the Arch of Triumph, and down the Champs-Elysee. Three days later, Hitler made a three-hour tour of the city. His henchmen stayed much longer, though, and established Nazi rule over Paris. The infrastructure and networks they built reflect the global system Hitler would

1. Joshua 1:3.

have established had he won the war and convey some idea of what a global order under an antichrist might look like.

After Paris fell, the Nazi flag was everywhere. Larry Collins and Dominique LaPierre write that it was the "symbol of the regime that...for four years shackled the spirit of the world's most beautiful city."[2] The French flag was locked away in a glass cabinet in the Army Museum of Les Invalides, fit only as a relic of the past. The Germans tore down 200 handsome bronze statues, hauled them off to Germany, and melted them down for weapons. Guard houses and pill boxes popped up all over the city. A French collaborationist newspaper was appropriately titled, *Je Suis Partout*—"I Am Everywhere."

German replaced French on street signs. French culture was undermined. Many of the city's great art treasures were locked away from public view or stolen outright. Parisian citizens had to carry identification papers wherever they went. Nazi rules and regulations were harshly enforced. Hitler demanded absolute control of the nations he conquered. He wanted total authority over the people—body, soul, and spirit. In every way possible they were subdued and crushed under the Nazi boot.

Hitler sought to create a global empire, which is impossible to maintain without a complex infrastructure. Such a system must regulate the economy, control communications and public opinion, and possess the power to enforce its decrees.

2. Larry Collins and Dominique LaPierre, *Is Paris Burning?* (New York: Simon and Schuster, 1965), 15.

The Old Testament Book of Daniel reveals four basic types of empires and the systems that make them work. There have been many empires throughout human history. Historian Arnold Toynbee has identified more than 20 historic civilizations. In one way or another, all have been variations of one or more of the four basic types described in Daniel.

Daniel chapter 2 records a dream experienced by Nebuchadnezzar, king of Babylon, in which he saw a huge statue with a head of gold, arms and breasts of silver, stomach and thighs of bronze, legs of iron, and feet of clay. A large stone crushed the clay feet, ground all the metals to dust, then grew to the size of a mountain and replaced the statue. The prophet Daniel interpreted the king's dream as referring to four earthly empires, from top to bottom progressively inferior in quality, and all eventually crushed and overcome by the Kingdom of God, the only true global empire. The four human empires share the same worldly life-source and values, and each possesses particular characteristics. These characteristics can be expected to appear in the global system sought by the antichrist spirit. The empires and characteristics as revealed in Nebuchadnezzar's dream are shown through the following:

Babylon: Empire of human messianism
Persia: Empire of militarism
Greece: Empire through cultural dominance
Rome: Empire through elitist dominance

Babylon: Empire of Human Messianism

One of the most significant features for which the Babylonian empire is remembered is architectural grandeur.

Temples, palaces, and public buildings filled the city. The Hanging Gardens at Nebuchadnezzar's palace were considered one of the Seven Wonders of the ancient world.

The distinctive mark of Babylonian architecture, however, was the ziggurat. These stone obelisks were high places for worship, religious rituals, and probably astrology. Many of these "stairways to the gods" have been unearthed in ancient Mesopotamia. John H. Walton writes of them:

> "The ziggurat was a structure that was built to support the stairway...which was believed to be used by the gods to travel from one realm to the other. It was solely for the convenience of the gods and was maintained in order to provide the deity with the amenities that would refresh him along the way ... The stairway led at the top to the gate of the gods, the entrance to the divine abode."[3]

The biblical Tower of Babel was most likely a ziggurat.

Babylon, or *Bab-Ilu*, means the "gate of the gods." Centuries later, Jesus would declare Himself to be the Door by which people came to God, but Babylon pretended to that role from the beginning. In her attempt to build a tower to the heavens in defiance of God, Babylon sought to restore paradise on man's terms rather than God's. Babylon, then, represents human messianism, or the belief that man is his own savior. Human messianism believes that man can

3. John H. Walton, *Bulletin for Biblical Research 5* (Associates for Biblical Research, 1996), 155-75.

erect his own route to God. All human-based religion arises from this impulse. The Bible reveals that man cannot find God, but that God must reveal Himself. Yet man pieces together religious systems with intricate rituals and works, in order to find God on his own. The work of Messiah is to reveal God to man and reconcile man to God. In seeking to do this himself, man becomes his own messiah, and eventually worships himself.

Human messianism also tries to place God at man's disposal. God must walk man's "stairway." He must come to man on man's terms. The true God comes on His own terms, or not at all.

Finally, human messianism attempts to set the parameters for interaction with God. Only the observable and quantifiable are real; there is no possibility of something "outside" the range of knowledge man has established.

Thus, humanism is represented by Babel, but its roots go back to Eden. Adam and Eve fell into sin because they wanted to be "like God," and sought their own means to achieve it. This urge of man to "play God" has been around ever since. Os Guinness, identifying milestones of humanism in history, writes that in Greece in the fifth century B.C., objective reason caused a separation of science and philosophy from religion and superstition. Later, during the Renaissance, man became the measure of all things. The Enlightenment and Age of Reason followed until, finally, the apex was reached in modern times with the consolidation of humanist associations and organizations.[4]

4. Os Guinness, *The Dust of Death* (Downers Grove: InterVarsity Press, 1973).

The *credo* of modern humanism is the *Humanist Manifesto*, written in 1933 and revised in 1973. Although the two versions differ in many respects, both avow the belief that "traditional theism, especially faith in the prayer-hearing God, assumed to love and care for persons, to hear and understand their prayers, and to be able to do something about them, is an unproved and outmoded faith."[5] In the spirit of Babylon, the *Humanist Manifesto II* asserts that "we begin with humans not God, nature, not deity." Man is the only available savior. "No deity will save us; we must save ourselves."

This philosophy is now lived out in practical application throughout the world. The humanist vision is truly that of global empire. "We have reached a turning point in human history where the best option is to *transcend the limits of national sovereignty* and to move toward the building of a world community in which all sectors of the human family can participate."[6] This would be accomplished through "a system of world law and a world order based on transnational federal government."

The signers of *Humanist Manifesto II* doubtless see the establishment of this world government and the empire of humanism, as a voluntary, happily embraced sovereignty, accepted by a world grateful to be rescued from chaos. Such a view is naive in the extreme. No such global empire

5. Paul Kurtz, "Humanist Manifesto II," *The Humanist*, vol. XXXIII, no. 5, Sep./Oct. 1973.
6. Emphasis is part of original quotation.

would be possible without stern militarism, which is the type of empire symbolized by the ancient Persians.

Persia: Empire of Militarism

In Nebuchadnezzar's dream, the silver arms and chest of the statue represent the empire of the Medes and Persians. Daniel 7:5 pictures this empire as a bear with three ribs dangling from its mouth, symbolizing its brute strength. The bear is told: "Arise, devour much meat!" which is exactly what it does.

J.M. Cook writes that "[e]fficiency in military preparations and frightening skills had given the Medes and Persians a reputation for invincibility."[7] Cyrus II brought the Persian empire to its greatest glory by unleashing a fierceness that overwhelmed other kingdoms, like Babylon, although Cyrus himself was gracious to those he defeated. By the time of Esther, the Persian Empire ranged from India to Ethiopia, and encompassed 127 provinces. King Ahasuerus held a festival in his capital, Susa, to which he invited his nobles and military leaders, as well as the princes of the provinces under Persian rule. It took 180 days for them to observe the display of "the riches of his royal glory and the splendor of his great majesty."[8]

The Persians descended from the Indo-Aryans and as early as 2000 B.C. settled in what is now Iran (a name derived from "Aryan"), along the Black Sea. Later, Hitler embraced

7. J.M. Cook, "Persia," *The Oxford Companion to the Bible* (New York: Oxford University Press, 1993), p. 583.
8. Esther 1:1-4.

Aryan myth as the basis for his racial views. From the beginning, the Aryans displayed an empiristic bent. They penetrated many cultures and societies. They were also noted for their savagery. Despite their brutality, however, they knew how to learn from and improve upon the achievements of their enemies, particularly in weaponry. All these characteristics flowed into the Persian peoples and the empire they created. Persian might was strong enough to maintain peace, and plan and implement sophisticated government.

The Persian-Aryan strain of empirism has been seen in the world throughout history. As Babylon was the fountainhead of human messianism, so Persia stands at the headwaters of militarism. This rumbling river has surged across the nations with devastating might. This has been especially true in the twentiethth century. In this century's wars, 33 million young men between the ages of 18 and 30 have perished. Zbigniew Brzezinski estimates that a total of 87 million people have been slaughtered in twentieth century conflicts.[9]

People in every generation take note of the dangerous militaristic trends of history, and try to do something about war. At that point, the Babylonian strain of empirism mingles with the Persian, and man decides he is the messiah who can solve the war problem. The nineteenth century, buoyed by the rationalistic optimism of the Enlightenment, developed the notion that the relationships of nations were guided by clear and well-understood rules

9. Zbigniew Brzezinski, *Out of Control* (New York: Charles Scribner's Sons, 1993), 10.

like those of chess. There seemed to be a fading of the warlike impulse in Europe that had nothing to do with religion, spirituality, or morality, but "to the progress of knowledge and intellectual activity."[10]

The fragile state of this optimism became terribly evident in 1914, when nations that had believed themselves to be in harmony found themselves in sharp dissonance. The natural response to the horror of World War I was despair. If confidence in human progress was misplaced, where then was the hope? This bleakness deteriorated into outright nihilism by the end of World War II.

Where now does humanity turn for salvation? Ironically, he looks to a depleted humanism, dressed in flashy new garb, that debuted in the Golden Age of Athens.

Greece: Empire Through Cultural Dominance

The bronze stomach and thighs of the statue in Nebuchadnezzar's dream represent the Greek empire under Alexander the Great. The Golden Age of Greece was almost past when Alexander came to power, but Greek culture—art, philosophy, literature—abounded. It was Alexander's destiny to extend that culture into most of the world of his day.

Classically educated by Aristotle himself, and influenced by his father, Philip of Macedon, Alexander developed an appreciation for Greek culture. Philip himself united all Greece except Sparta under one rule, but died

10. Geoffrey Blainey, *The Causes of War* (New York: The Free Press, 1973), 20.

two years later. Upon becoming ruler of Greece, Alexander lost no time in expanding his empire. First came the Persians. Moving swiftly across the Hellespont to the Granicus River, Alexander defeated a Persian army four times the size of his own. In 331 B.C. he defeated Darius and was declared "king of Asia." Babylon and even the Persian capital of Susa opened to him all their treasure and wealth. Alexander pressed eastward, to India, and was halted only by the weariness of his own army.

In Daniel 7:6, Greece appears as a leopard. This is not surprising in light of Alexander's tactics. Persia's military strategy was based on conquest by sheer numbers. Alexander, on the other hand, used speed and cunning. When Alexander died at the age of 33, in 323 B.C., he was master of a domain stretching from Egypt to India.

What kind of empire did Alexander establish? Aristotle taught that the world was divided between Greeks and Barbarians. "The essential feature of Greek civilization," wrote Lionel Curtis, "was the state, through the medium of which the fullest development of human faculties was alone attainable."[11] It was that civilization that Alexander extended into his world.

Greek culture emphasized the individual and deified man, in fact, if not in principle. If the world of untouchable, frightening gods was transcendence in its terrifying extreme, Grecian individualism was immanence taken to

11. Lionel Curtis, *Civitas Dei: The Commonwealth of God* (London: Macmillan and Co. Limited, 1938), 82.

its limits. The human being became the object of worship. Babylonian humanism was the pedestal on which Greece erected the graven image of the human being. The gods and goddesses of the Greeks, says Michael Grant, were "human beings writ large, because the Greeks, with their lively dramatic and plastic sense, were so conscious of the potentialities of men and women that they could not imagine the deities in any other shape."[12]

The Greek gods reflected the human world and were subject to human foibles. Divinity centered on human form provides a natural platform on which to raise up man as a god. The centerpiece of Greek culture, which Alexander spread throughout his empire, was the human being—his wisdom, creativity and appearance.

According to Albert Speer, Hitler believed that "the culture of the Greeks had reached the peak of perfection in every field."[13] One day, as Hitler lingered over the photo of a beautiful young female swimmer, he said, "What splendid bodies you see today. It is only in our century that young people have once again approached Hellenistic ideals through sports." He would have thought himself a prophet could he have visited the spas, health clubs, and recreation centers that today serve as modern temples to the human body.

Influenced as he was by the Aryan myth and Greek culture, Hitler's hatred of the Jews, the crippled, the mentally

12. Michael Grant, *The Rise of the Greeks* (New York: Charles Scribner's Sons, 1987), 17.
13. Albert Speer, *Inside the Third Reich* (New York: The Macmillan Company, 1970), 115.

handicapped, and the ugly was logical. The Jews, the lame and the weak failed to measure up to Aryan standards. Hitler and the Nazis were not the first. Hermann Ahlwardt, a member of the German Parliament in the late nineteenth century, wrote *The War of Desperation Between the Aryan Peoples and Judaism*, in which he states, "The people which rids itself of its Jews first and most radically and thus frees the way for the natural development of its culture, will be summoned to be the bearers of culture and, consequently, also to be the ruler of the world."[14]

There can be little doubt that America today is a modern "bearer of culture" to the world. The Greek strain of empirism abounds throughout modern America. American fashions, technology, music, and all other kinds of goods and services are in high demand all over the world. Some of this cultural export is positive and healthy, and other cultures assimilate it with no harm. Other elements of America's cultural influence are questionable. In fact, there is growing concern about America's cultural export. Violence, unleashed sex, and just plain tackiness trouble many.

America once had a noble vision regarding its global cultural mission. The messianic sense has long been a part of the American psyche. In 1900, for example, Senator Albert J. Beveridge declared that "God's hand" was in America's expansion overseas. God's plan was working out the "glorious result" of America's global spread. It was, in fact,

14. Horst Von Malitz, *The Evolution of Hitler's Germany* (New York: McGraw-Hill, 1973), 78-79.

"futile" to resist "the continuance today of the American people toward the mastery of the world. This is a destiny neither vague nor undesirable. It is definite, splendid and holy." Sixty-one years later, John F. Kennedy picked up the same theme in his inaugural speech. "The energy, the faith, the devotion which we bring to this endeavor will light our country and all who serve it, and the glow from the fire can truly light the world."

No doubt Beveridge and Kennedy wanted to "light the world" with the best of America. For many, that "best" was America's spiritual bedrock—the gospel of Jesus Christ—and the governing form emerging from it, democracy in a representative system of checks and balances. This is deeply rooted in America's past. The idea was summed up neatly by John Winthrop, first governor of the Massachusetts Bay Colony. "We must consider that we shall be as a City upon a Hill, the eyes of all people...upon us." Thus America became the world's greatest missionary nation, planting the gospel throughout the globe. Many would argue that America's unusual material bounty was given to enable the nation to carry out its missionary destiny.

Now, of course, the Greek idea of empirism has replaced Biblical evangelism. New elites have arisen to define what is "American," and a fierce culture war is under way to prevent the elites from spreading their tyranny. The outcome of that war will affect not only the United States, but also all who lie within the scope of her cultural empire.

Rome: Empire Through Elitist Dominance

The fourth empire in Nebuchadnezzar's dream was Rome, represented on the statue by legs of iron. Daniel 7:7

presents Rome as a horrible, powerful beast with iron teeth that crushes all the other kingdoms.

Rome, influenced by Greek culture, rose to an empire as peasants under the leadership of an oligarchy. It first conquered Italy and then the Mediterranean, including Greece herself. According to Dionysius of Halicarnassus, who arrived in Rome around 30 B.C. and taught there for two decades, Rome was "the first and the only State recorded in all time that ever made the risings and the settings of the sun the boundaries of her dominion."

One distinctive characteristic of the Roman Empire was its rule by an elitist aristocracy comprised of a core of families that persisted across generations. Until 510 B.C., Rome was led by kings. Then the monarchy was replaced by a dual headship of two consuls elected by an assembly of adult males under the counsel of former magistrates comprising the senate.

The Roman elite were of the Patrician class, a closed group of families that first arose during the monarchy, outlasted it, and continued to monopolize Roman institutions.[15] Roman government was directed by such hereditary elders for centuries. One of their major concerns was determining who actually qualified as "Romans." There was no question that all power resided in the people, but who were the people? For the Roman elite, the "people" were those who inherited the aristocracy, or moved into it

15. Michael Crawford, *The Roman Republic* (Cambridge: Harvard University Press, 1993), 24.

through a series of specific steps. *Libertas*, or freedom, was identified with *civitas*, citizenship. A slave or foreign-born person would not enjoy the full benefits of freedom in the Roman empire. On the other hand, Roman citizenship conveyed considerable benefits, as the apostle Paul discovered.[16] When a citizen performed great services to the state, he was endowed with *dignitas*, standing, reputation, which granted him *autoritas*, or influence. So, in Rome, elite status came through blood.

Blood, property, and achievement are the ways people attain elitist status in various modern societies, according to German sociologist Karl Mannheim.[17] Of Mannheim's conclusion, Robert Bork says, "Aristocratic society chose elites primarily on the blood principle; bourgeois society on the property principle; modern democracy has stressed the achievement principle."[18]

Elitists seek to control and shape public opinion and policy according to what they believe is in the public's general interest. Those who disagree with them do not deserve to have a voice in the public forum. So, the elitists try to silence or discredit those opposing voices. Today's elites decide what is in the general interest, based on their own standard of values, and only that which conforms is allowed expression. This is the meaning of political correctness.

16. Acts 22:25-29.
17. Quoted by Robert Bork in *Slouching Towards Gomorrah* (New York: Regan Books, 1996), 78.
18. Quoted by Bork, *Slouching Towards*, 78.

There are three elitist groups who exert an imperial hold on the modern United States. The first is the media-entertainment complex. There is a growing concern among many Americans, conservative and liberal alike, that the news and entertainment media are heavily biased toward liberal views and attitudes. William A. Rusher believes that it is not simply an unfair bias, but a "fundamental problem of the distribution of forces within American society."[19]

The second dominant American elite is the academic community. Professor Allan Bloom writes of its power, "What is influential in the higher intellectual circles always ends up in the schools."[20] The influence of this elite on the culture is pervasive. Robert Bork notes that "because they wield the power of language and symbols, their values and ideas are broadcast by the press, movies, television, universities, primary and secondary schools, books and magazines, philanthropies, foundations and many churches. Thus, intellectuals are influential out of all proportion to their numbers."[21]

The third elitist group influencing America is egalitarian-populist politicians and movements. Egalitarianism is the idea that everyone should enjoy an equal measure of outcome, irrespective of contribution, or, "the equality of

---

19. William A. Rusher, *The Coming Battle for the Media* (New York: William Morrow and Company, Inc., 1988).
20. Allan Bloom, *The Closing of the American Mind* (New York: Simon and Shuster, 1985), 55.
21. Bork, *Slouching Towards*, 84.

outcomes rather than of opportunities."[22] Populism is politics by polls. It is discovering what people want and constructing campaigns emphasizing those desires above the real, and sometimes painful, needs of society.

Two of the three elites are almost untouchable. The media-entertainment complex and academia submit to no one. The media, when challenged, falls back on "the people's right to know" and the importance of a free press. Those who criticize the entertainment side are accused of censorship and of trying to squelch freedom of expression. Meanwhile, the elites continue to suppress whomever they wish through selective exclusion from the public gateways in which they sit. Challengers of the academic elite are labeled tyrants who wish to halt freedom of thought.

The interconnectedness of these four basic empires is shown by their appearing in Nebuchadnezzar's dream as one massive statue. Each is a part of the others, and each one incorporates the characteristics of its predecessor, but in ever-decreasing quality as far as the dynamics of the Kingdom of God are concerned. Since the last three rise from the humanist head of Babylon, Babylon then becomes the prime symbol of the world system. Likewise, the global system sought by the antichrist spirit is a combination of these four fundamental empires. It is humanistic, militaristic, culturally dominant, and elitist.

The "Babylonian" World System

The Book of Revelation depicts the approaching world system with two powerful images: a horrible beast arising

22. Bork, *Slouching Towards*, 5.

from the sea, having seven heads, ten horns, and full of blasphemous names, resembling a leopard, but with the feet of a bear and mouth of a lion,[23] and as a harlot, drunk with the blood of the saints, sitting astride the horrible beast,[24]. The harlot is identified as "Babylon," and both she and the beast represent the antichristian world system and the satanic power behind it.

The imperial powers of the four representative empires that merge to form the one world system are tenacious. It is vital that the "Normandy"-minded church recognize the characteristics of this "Babylonian" world system and be prepared to do battle in the power of the Spirit with the forces of evil that lie behind it. This world system seeks dominance over humanity in three main areas: politics, religion, and economics.

Politics

Humanity, in its spiritual blindness and rebellion, cries out for a savior as global cultural, social, and moral problems multiply. Characteristically, the Babylonian world system presents itself as the answer to these problems. The "beast" in Revelation 13 resembled a leopard, sleek, cunning, beautiful. Likewise, the Babylonian system will appear to the world, through effective use and manipulation of the media, in very attractive packaging, seducing the masses, desperate for solutions to world problems, to embrace it. As discussed earlier, this is already beginning to

23. Revelation 13:1ff.
24. Revelation 18:1ff.

happen as world leaders position themselves in favor of humanistically-based global solutions that transcend national boundaries.

The humanistic cultural values of this system become more and more pervasive worldwide as the brightest and best in each society are tempted to embrace them. Political leaders, journalists, academicians, and even religious leaders become advocates of these values and are instrumental in passing them down to the rest of the population.

As its power and influence grow, the Babylonian system is not hesitant to use war or the threat of war to accomplish its purposes. This war-making capability is symbolized by the bear-like feet of the beast in Revelation 13. Even today there is increasing use of international "peace-keeping" forces under the auspices of the UN attempting to bring stability to hot spots such as Bosnia. Although the official role of these units is keeping the peace, the threat of war is certainly there.

The Babylonian world system becomes increasingly arrogant in its humanistic approach to mankind's problems. The beast of Revelation 13 had the "mouth of a lion." Through this mouth, Babylon utters blasphemies against God. The values of this world system are completely opposed to those of God. Great pressure is applied to all people to conform to the values preached by the world system. In this environment, the only true "enemy" is the "true believer," the one who insists that there are absolute values and takes a firm public stand for them. This lies behind the current battle to remove the voice of the Church from the public forum for the sake of maintaining "separation of church and state."

Religion

Because of the pervasiveness of the religious impulse in man worldwide, control and regulation of it is vital for the Babylonian world system. The only spirituality it can accept is the kind it can control. Religion, then, is a powerful weapon in Babylon's arsenal to deceive and control the people. There is no room for any faith or belief system with exclusive claims—such as Christianity. The religion of the Babylonian world system is humanistically based and seeks the lowest common denominator among the world's people. That is, it is inclusive and universal, encompassing everyone. Its only sacrament is that of complete conformity to the system.

The world of the occult plays a vital role in the religious structure of Babylon. Occultic deception is pervasive in society, as seen in the popularity of horoscopes, fortune tellers, crystals, and the like. It is ironic that occultic practices are very strong even in the most sophisticated secular societies. Counterfeit "signs" of spiritual power, actually demonic activity, occur to dazzle and amaze people and deceive them into acknowledging the reality and power of Babylon's religious system. In overtly occult societies, such "signs" are common, and they are becoming more frequent in other societies as well.

Economics

Another crucial area of control for the Babylonian system is global economics. There is economic disarray in many parts of the world. This is seen in the rise of deficit spending, the prevalence of unchecked greed, and in binding interdependence between nations. The Babylonian system promises to solve all this with a globally based economy. As this economic system becomes more widespread and nations "buy" into it, eventually it will become a means of controlling behavior. In such a system, buying or selling is dependent on conformity to the system and its values. The technology for this kind of control exists today. Electronic commerce, buying and selling over the Internet, is one example. Putting microchips in credit cards is another. Such chips would record personal information about the cardholder that would be needed in transactions. Once such electronic commerce becomes the primary or only means of doing business, the consumer will have no control over the information he provides.

Like large vines twirling around one another, politics, religion, and economics make up a system that seems incapable of being uprooted. These tangles are used masterfully by the occupier to choke the nations. The only hope is for intervention from outside the occupied world—the blessed invasion.

Chapter 5

The Unfolding Battle

Hitler's global plans began to unravel when his systems could no longer support the extent of empire he envisioned. Germany's invasion of the Soviet Union was the beginning of the end for Hitler. Early victories were stalled by Germany's inability to establish and maintain adequate systems of supply and control. Delayed by logistic problems, the Germans were caught in the harsh Russian winter, which helped to end their advance.

Transportation was one of the most vital systems because the steady flow of supplies depended on it. In France, the Germans took advantage of the extensive French railroad system. It is only logical, then, that Allied plans for the Normandy invasion included destruction of the French railway network.

On April 14, 1944, General Eisenhower assumed leadership of the strategic air forces as part of his total command. He issued orders for attacks on the transportation system. First, deplete the Luftwaffe and demolish its bases. Second, "destroy and disrupt the enemy's rail communications, particularly those affecting movements toward the 'OVERLORD' lodgment area." Prior to D-Day, 5,000 tons of bombs were dropped on the Germans' strategic rail centers, and with the help of the French resistance, by D-Day the transportation system was at the point of total collapse.[1]

Between March 1 and June 6, 1944 rail traffic declined 60 per cent. This would prove critical in the battle for Normandy.[2]

The Kingdom of God was planted in occupied earth with the incarnation of Jesus Christ as certainly as the Allied victory was seeded in occupied Europe with the Normandy invasion. In both cases, a beachhead was established, leading to the securing of bridgeheads, then to the linking of forces for a total victory.

A beachhead is a secured position, or lodgment, on a beach for the purpose of driving inland against an enemy. A bridgehead is a fortified point established by an invading force on the enemy's side of a bridge, river, or gap. A beachhead is pointless without a bridgehead. Dunkirk was not a beachhead because it anticipated withdrawal rather than advance. Normandy was a beachhead. The next step was establishing the bridgehead.

---

1. Gordon A. Harrison, *United States Army in World War II, The European Theater of Operations, Cross-Channel Attack* (New York: Barnes and Noble Books, 1995), 224.
2. Harrison, *European Theater*, 230.

When Jesus Christ came into the world as God incarnate, He established the beachhead of God's Kingdom. The next phase was planting a solid Kingdom bridgehead. The strategic plan for Allied advance after Normandy contains parallels to the unfolding plan for the advance of God's Kingdom in the earth.

The beachhead at Normandy was established when Allied troops poured ashore from 5,000 ships onto five beaches along 50 miles of Normandy coastline. The German resistance was strongest at Omaha Beach, where Americans took many casualties before seizing high ground and securing the beachhead. There is no more perilous period of battle than the initial assault. The first soldiers on the Normandy beaches not only faced rifle and artillery fire from the slopes above, but also minefields. By the evening of June 6, 1944, 10,000 Allied soldiers had been killed, captured, or wounded.

Jesus Christ's coming into the world was the "first wave" of the Kingdom invasion. He met fierce, violent resistance when He arrived and began preaching and ministering the Kingdom of God.

The works and ideas of the Kingdom are alien and threatening to the world controlled by the adversary. Jesus was the first to speak and do the works of the Kingdom. Like the Nazi soldiers caught by surprise at Normandy, the enemy was shocked when the Kingdom invaded a domain the destroyer thought he had secured. And, like the first wave landing at Normandy, Jesus took the full brunt of the enemy's determined resistance. The cross was the result. But the cross was also the defeat of the evil one.

Converting a beachhead into a bridgehead involves concentration of personnel and equipment.

A major priority for Eisenhower and his commanders was control of air and sea lanes between the English bases and the Normandy coast. This maintained the flow of men and material. It was also important to block the Nazi supply lines. The Allies carried out major bombing raids on roads, rails, ports, terminals, and depots. There was internal sabotage against these critical German supply points. The French resistance ambushed and destroyed the enemy's resource links.

It is vital that the advancing Church not only intercede for the "open heaven," but that she also does warfare against enemy supply lines. This means locating points where the adversary is able to pour his resources into the world. Spiritual mapping is crucial for understanding where these supply lines are. Individual followers of Christ must be continually aware of places in their lives where the enemy can gain ground. Personal repentance and spiritual warfare concentrated on the enemy's control points are critical.

Pentecost is the bridgehead for the Kingdom invasion. The supply lines of Heaven are open to the battlefield on earth. Obstacles to power in ministry are removed. Kingdom works occur, the back of the enemy is broken, and the harvest sweeps in.

From Pentecost, the blessed invasion moves out with a mighty army, the Church, to carry victory into the heart of enemy territory. That army is equipped with an unbeatable arsenal: the power of the Holy Spirit and prayer to keep the supply lines open. The Holy Spirit also unifies the Church to work together to accomplish the mission. When the Spirit came down at Pentecost, the disciples were all together "in one accord." In that moment, the Spirit welded them into a single front to move against the enemy.

Following the beachhead and the bridgehead is the critical "breakout" phase. At the Normandy coast, the Allies faced a countryside full of hedgerows and mushy terrain, where the Germans hoped to trap them. But the Allies cut roads through dunes and other barriers and moved forward.

Long ago, God made a promise to His people regarding the opening of the way to victory:

> *Thus says the Lord, who makes a way through the sea and a path through the mighty waters, who brings forth the chariot and the horse, the army and the mighty man (they will lie down together and not rise again; they have been quenched and extinguished like a wick): "Do not call to mind the former things, or ponder things of the past. Behold, I will do something new, now it will spring forth; will you not be aware of it? I will even make a roadway in the wilderness, rivers in the desert"* (Isaiah 43:16-19).

God's promise was that there would be a "highway" for His people[3]. Above all, there would be the forerunner who would call out, "Clear the way for the Lord in the wilderness; make smooth in the desert a highway for our God." And "...every mountain and hill be made low; and let the

3. Isaiah 11:16.

rough ground become a plain, and the rugged terrain a broad valley; then the glory of the Lord will be revealed, and all flesh will see it together; for the mouth of the Lord has spoken."[4] As the Church proclaims the Kingdom and does its work, she opens the roads and routes that enable breakout.

This means penetrating the many facets of a city. It involves opening roads for the Kingdom into homes and families, into the marketplace and workplace, into political and government establishments, and into the educational system. As the Church penetrates these key areas of life with the message and works of the Kingdom, breakout will occur.

If Pentecost is the bridgehead for the blessed invasion, Reformation is the breakout phase. Prior to the Reformation, the Church had become bogged down in ritual, worldliness, ignorance, and doctrinal error. She had lost sight of her empowerment by the Holy Spirit. Finally, she forgot how to use the awesome armaments she had been given under the open heaven. Physical wars against human enemies were substituted for the deeply pitched spiritual warfare fought by the New Testament Church.

The Reformation settled the issue of authority. Under the popes, church and state became as one, with the institutional authority of the church at the center. That authority defined the battlefield, the enemy, and the weapons to be used. When Martin Luther and the other Reformers

4. Isaiah 40:3-5.

cried for *sola Scriptura* ("only Scripture") as the sole authority for faith and practice in the Church, they challenged false, nonbiblical authority based upon men and institutions.

The Reformation shattered the institutional wrappings that had obscured even the potential for Spirit-empowered ministry. The explosive awakenings and movements of later centuries would have been impossible without the Reformation.

God brought about the Reformation "in the fulness of time." The Renaissance reawakened man's hunger for knowledge. The Reformation stirred his thirst for the Word of God. The invention of the printing press made the Bible available to the masses for the first time, and, because of the work of courageous translators, in a language they could understand.

After the breakout comes the period of strategic advance. For the Allies at Normandy, this meant taking key cities, and then pressing forward into Nazi-held France. Entire regions were controlled from the cities. That's why capturing them was so important. Liberating the cities would lead to liberating the nation. The strategic port city of Cherbourg was captured on June 27, 1944. St. Lo, a crossroads town in western Normandy, was another vital target. Patton's Third Army swept south, then east, and linked up with other Allied forces at the River Seine. This opened the way to Paris. The Allies captured St. Lo on July 18, 1944, and the entire western front opened up.

The Church moves from breakout to strategic advance when she seriously identifies and assaults the critical strongholds of the enemy, the "cities" of concentrated demonic presence by which whole territories are dominated. Local churches are in a position for strategic advance when their vision expands beyond their specific locations to encompass their entire cities. Strategic advance will occur as individual congregations join others in the common task of defeating the adversary and his strongholds in their city. There were many obstacles to the linking of the Allied powers at Normandy. The British and Americans had major tactical differences. Polish, Free French, Canadian, and other units had every reason to stand off from one another. They came together, though, in the interests of defeating a common foe. This same attitude is essential for the Church if strategic advance is to progress.

Spiritually, the Bible presents the reality of two "cities": Jerusalem and Babylon. Jerusalem symbolizes the Kingdom of God, the dominion of life and light. Babylon is the type of the world system, controlled by the kingdom of death and darkness. Thus, the Church in strategic advance will be striking at the world system itself. This means the Church will neither ignore nor isolate herself from systemic evil. She will speak prophetically against it; she will pray strategically against it; she will proclaim the Kingdom of God positively in the face of it. She will not remain in a religious ghetto or stained-glass compound. The Church in strategic advance will be "out there" in the world, challenging demonic structures of spiritual and physical oppression, injustice, deceit, and death. The Church in strategic advance will be as determined to storm the gates of Babylon as were the Allies in their determination to win Cherbourg.

If Pentecost marks the establishment of the bridgehead, and the Reformation that of the breakout phase, then the age beginning with the Great Awakenings, which has continued in the Pentecostal-Charismatic renewals, signals the period of strategic advance. This is the present stage of the blessed invasion.

When Eisenhower was named Supreme Commander of the Allied forces, he pulled together the best planning team he could muster. Churchill was worried about many aspects of D-Day. "I knew that it would be a very heavy and hazardous adventure," he wrote.[5] Therefore, precise planning was essential. Throughout the summer of 1943—a year before the invasion—the Allied Inter-Service Staff worked intensely on the plan. It had to include training, invasion site selection, logistical support, weather trends, tide tables, and countless other items.

At points, the planning was masterful. One element, for example, was planning how to keep the enemy from knowing the place and time of the invasion and causing the Germans to think the assault would come somewhere else at a different time. The planning and execution of this facet of "Overlord" brought a final result that was, in Churchill's words, "admirable."[6]

However, no matter how masterful the planning, without fire power the plan would be useless. At some point,

5. Harrison, *European Theater*, 804.
6. Harrison, *European Theater*, 807.

the plan for warfare had to be linked to the weapons of warfare. The cognitive "brain work" had to be joined to the power of the attack itself. The key was linking the cognitive element with the power element. Artillery without planning would result in wasted weapons, fired randomly. Planning without the power of the weapons would simply be a war game and would have no effect on the enemy.

This is why the Reformation had to be linked with the intensified movements of the Holy Spirit, beginning with the Great Awakenings of the eighteenth century in Europe and America. The Pentecostal-Charismatic renewals have constituted the continuing barrage. The most concentrated combination of spiritual power comes as the Word of God is tied in ministry and application to the Spirit of God. The Bible enables the Church to identify the plan of attack; the Spirit empowers the Church to do the warfare. If a church is closed to the present-day ministry of the Spirit, it spends all its time on the cognitive planning phase. It studies the plan, analyzes it, meditates on it, discusses it, but rarely moves on to warfare. Any church that embraces the Spirit but tries to war without the Word is like an army trying to go up against a well-organized enemy without a plan of attack. It is when Word and Spirit are linked that the strategic advance accelerates.

This is also the point at which the enemy fights back with desperate resistance. Hitler himself devised a strategy to exploit what even the Allies themselves recognized as a weakness in their plan of advance. The Allied offensive in Europe called for armies surging south through France and north, then linking at the River Seine. This strategy, however, left the center weak. Hitler decided to send as powerful a force as he could muster through that center, which was in the Ardennes, in Belgium, then pivot his armies to the north and northwest to sever the Allied armies and take Antwerp, whose port was supplying the Allies in the north.

He almost succeeded. To the amazement of Allied leaders, Hitler amassed 70 divisions, 15 of which were armored. On December 16, 1944, he sent them forward, creating a "bulge" in the Allied lines, and giving the name to this phase of the conflict—the Battle of the Bulge. The timing and strength of the assault surprised the Allies. Ten days later, the German armies had pierced 60 miles into the Allied lines and were only four miles from their objective, the Meuse River. The soldiers were weary, and strong Allied counterattacks halted the advance.

Meanwhile, armies led by Patton and Montgomery closed in on the enemy from the south and north. They beat the Germans back, and by the end of December, Hitler's forces were back inside German borders, having suffered 120,000 casualties. It was the last great German offensive of the World War II. Churchill noted that, although it was a hard blow for the Allies, there were some definite benefits to this phase of the war. The Battle of the Bulge made subsequent fights easier because the Germans couldn't replace the men and material lost at the Bulge. It also possibly "disillusioned" the German High Command.[7]

7. Harrison, *European Theater*, 899.

The devil devises plans and traps to exploit weaknesses in the strategy of the advancing Church. As the Church moves toward final victory, the enemy throws everything he can muster against her.

In Revelation 16, God pours out His wrath on the earthly powers that have opposed Him, in the form of the "bowl judgments." In the midst of unveiling the miseries man's rebellion has triggered, the Lord speaks to the Church. "Behold," says the Christ, "I am coming like a thief. Blessed is the one who stays awake and keeps his garments, lest he walk about naked and men see his shame."[8] Specifically, the Lord is warning His people about the enemy's ability to deceive. Through deception, the adversary and his allies are drawing the earthly powers to Armageddon for the show-down in which they will be ripped to pieces. The people of God can be caught in the seduction of the enemy if they are not alert. In Matthew 24:24 Jesus warns, "For false Christs and false prophets will arise and will show great signs and wonders, so as to mislead, if possible, even the elect."

Thus, the advancing Church must watch for delusion and stay alert, lest she be led astray. She must realize that the enemy, although ultimately defeated, still has deadly power and will strike in desperation with all his remaining might.

The strategic advance leads to the point of crossing over into the enemy's home territory. This is the domain

8. Revelation 16:15.

from which he controls all that he has conquered. It is the realm the adversary possesses and where he has his throne. In the case of World War II, this, of course, was Germany. Following the Battle of the Bulge, the Allies pursued the Nazis into their own country. To do so, they had to cross the natural barrier of the Rhine River.

As the U.S.First Army's Ninth Armored Division approached the bridge at Remagen, they discovered it damaged but passable. Four divisions were able to cross into German territory and establish a bridgehead inside Hitler's domain. Patton pounded the enemy to the south, and, after six weeks of bloody struggle on a 250-mile front, the enemy's home base was penetrated.

The advancing Church must also look for bridges into the enemy's heartland. When they are found, she must aggressively move over them. Such bridges will be the manifestations in society of the enemy's total control. One of the things that will distinguish a church in strategic advance from others is that such a Church will be crossing and penetrating where others have not gone.

The Church in strategic advance is like that of Rome, in Paul's day. Paul closes his letter to the Philippian believers with the salutation that the saints in Rome saluted them, especially the "saints" in Caesar's household.[9] This meant the Church had penetrated right into the ruler's inner chambers. So, the Church in strategic advance doesn't win just people who respond readily and easily, but also those who are key in the enemy's plans and actions.

9. Philippians 4:22.

Strangely, at least to the British, Eisenhower pulled back his armies from taking Berlin, leaving the city to fall to the Soviets. This decision complicated post-war international relations and brought the world to the edge of additional conflict. Doubtless Eisenhower knew taking Berlin would be costly to his men, but the pull-back left the bastion of the enemy open to the encroachment of another enemy.

The Church must learn the lesson. She must not pull away from the last, bitter battles, nor should she give her place to another. Each part of the Body of Christ has an important mission in the advance of the Kingdom. No part should relinquish his or her assignment to another. Each part has a "sphere of authority," and it's vital to the outcome of the war of the cosmos that every part of the Body know and function in its "measure."

Chapter 6

The Sphere of Authority

On December 5, 1943, President Franklin D. Roosevelt faced an immense dilemma. The final choice of a supreme commander for Operation Overlord, the Normandy invasion, had to be made. Winston Churchill had agreed earlier that an American would hold the post. Planning for the greatest invasion in history was stalled until Roosevelt made his decision.

Churchill and everyone else assumed Roosevelt would name General George C. Marshall, Army Chief of Staff, to the post. In fact, Marshall was the preferred choice for both Churchill and Stalin, as well as Harry Hopkins, Roosevelt's chief confidant, and Henry Stimson, the Secretary of War. Roosevelt, however, needed Marshall in Washington. "I feel I could not sleep at night with you out of the country," he told the general. The command went to Eisenhower.

When Eisenhower arrived in London to assume command, he inherited an invasion plan fraught with tremendous problems. Nothing on such a scale had ever been attempted before. British General Frederick Morgan, one of the preliminary planners for Operation Overlord, believed that Eisenhower was the right man for the job. Even Montgomery, Eisenhower's ally and critic, later commented that he knew of

> "...no other person who could have welded the Allied forces into such a fine fighting machine in the way he did, and kept a balance among the many conflicting and disturbing elements which threatened at times to wreck the ship."[1]

Dwight David Eisenhower was the man for the hour. Ike had found his place.

Successful Kingdom advance depends on warriors who have found their "place." The "Normandy"-minded church knows it has a destiny and moves in it. Eisenhower was in Italy when his appointment to Supreme Commander was announced. He bade farewell to the armies in Italy, "until we meet again in the heart of the enemy's Continental stronghold...." If the "Normandy"-minded church is to pierce into the heart of the enemy's stronghold, its people must understand they have a specific place in time and space, related to the cosmic war.

This is because of the awesome plan of God. God is transcendent, and God is love. The God who is high and lifted up, eternal, invisible and immortal, clothed in mystery,

1. Norman Geib, *Ike and Monty: Generals at War* (New York: William Morrow and Co., 1994), 278.

is compelled by that love to communicate. Love is based on relationship; relationship is predicated upon communication. Therefore the transcendent One must become immanent in time and space.

Immanence means specificity, locality. That is, if God is perfectly immanent, He will not hover in an atmospheric cloud, but will manifest Himself to specific people at specific points in *space*. Abram, a son of pagan moon worshippers, met God at an oak tree at Shechem, in Canaan.[2] The same God appeared to Jacob in the same land.[3] This encounter with the transcendent One in time and space was so remarkable that each man erected an altar on the spot so the moment would never fade.

Hundreds of years later, Moses encountered God in a flaming bush. After that experience, Moses returned to Egypt and led the Israelites to freedom. Later, in the Sinai desert, God told Moses to build a tabernacle, a "tent of dwelling," and gave him precise instructions regarding its construction. There the presence of God would descend and the Almighty would literally dwell among His people.

The supreme realization of God's immanent presence is Jesus Christ. He is "Emmanuel"—"God with us."[4] In His incarnation, Jesus became the "tabernacle" of the nearness of the Most High.[5] Jesus is the "fulness of the Godhead

2. Genesis 12:6-7.
3. Genesis 35:6-7.
4. Matthew 1:23.
5. John 1:14.

bodily."[6] In His Incarnation, Jesus is the place in the world where God is immanently and manifestly present.

Immanence also means that God is Himself present in a specific *time* as well as place. Paul writes that God sent Christ in the "fulness of time."[7] In Greek, "fulness" is *pleroma*. The term presents the picture of a container being filled to the brim.

"Time" in Galatians 4:4 is *chronos*, meaning simply the passage of time, the ticking of the clock, the marking of the calendar. *Kairos* is a term translated "time," which means a period of opportunity, or destiny. So Christ comes in the "fulness of time," indicating that the "vessel" of aeons and ages was filled with hundreds of millions of individual moments, until all culminated in a grand *kairos*, the coming of Christ, which was the *pleroma* of time.

Just as all people in the Kingdom of God have a specific place of service, they also have a specific time for which they were created for ministry. As with Esther, someone could say of such people, "You have come into the kingdom for such a time as this."[8] They will discover that there is a period of time for which they are uniquely fashioned. Perhaps there is one person they are to encounter and lead into the Kingdom. Maybe there's a movement aborning for which they are to provide unique leadership and service. Their purpose may be simply to speak one word

6. Colossians 2:9.
7. Galatians 4:4.
8. See Esther 4:14.

that will lead to the destruction of a key enemy strategy. Such people understand that an entire life is worth living just to reach the *kairos* that comes in the flow of *chronos*, and they will say, "All my previous experience was preparation for what I'm doing now."

Winston Churchill had difficulty finding his "time." Prior to World War II, he had a full military and political career. When the war began, he had been out of political office for a number of years and had been one of the few strident voices warning Britain of the need to prepare herself for war. He was, however, England's "man of the hour" during the war, and he led the nation brilliantly. After victory was won, however, he was voted out of office by a people now more concerned with domestic issues. Churchill, who had wanted a part in shaping the post-war world, was deeply disappointed. There was a "time," however, for which he had been preserved—before and after that time his effectiveness was limited.

Before He ascended to the Father, Jesus told His disciples that they would do the same works they had witnessed Him do and greater.[9] He told them it was to their advantage that He leave, "for if I do not go away, the Helper shall not come to *you*."[10] When Jesus was baptized, the Spirit came to enable Him to carry out His powerful ministry of the Kingdom. Jesus' departure was crucial for the Spirit to also come on His followers and empower them.

9. John 14:12.
10. John 16:7.

The Church, made up of human "living stones" and indwelt by the presence and power of the Holy Spirit, continues Christ's incarnate, immanent ministry in time and space. This means that every Spirit-indwelt person has a specific place in space and time where the Father assigns him or her for Kingdom ministry. Sometimes, though, Kingdom people complain about their "orders." If they cannot see the full vision, or comprehend the overall plan, they have trouble understanding their role in it.

Jesus' disciples have a greater excitement about their "orders" when they realize they are part of a greater plan. In an army, individual units are assigned specific tasks, but only the top-level commanders see the whole picture. So it is in the Kingdom of God. God Himself knows the total scope of the war of the cosmos. He issues His "orders" to His people at all levels: comprehensive commands to the Church in general, as well as specific ministries and directives to the churches in a given city. As the apostle Paul writes, "But to each one is given the manifestation of the Spirit for the common good."[11]

Within the context of those "orders," the servants of the Kingdom have special authority and ability. Second Corinthians 10:13-16 explains:

> *But we will not boast beyond our measure, but within the measure of the sphere which God apportioned to us as a measure, to reach even as far as you. For we are not overextending ourselves, as if we did not reach to you, for we*

11. 1 Corinthians 12:7.

were the first to come even as far as you in the gospel of Christ; not boasting beyond our measure, that is, in other men's labors, but with the hope that as your faith grows, we shall be, within our sphere, enlarged even more by you, so as to preach the gospel even to the regions beyond you, and not to boast in what has been accomplished in the sphere of another.

"Measure" means "a determined extent," and "sphere," a "province," or the territory of special responsibility and authority.

When Eisenhower was made Supreme Commander, he was given a "province" where he had full authority. When the time came to decide whether or not to invade, it was to Eisenhower everyone looked, even Roosevelt and Churchill. It was Eisenhower's "measure" to determine the commitment of hundreds of thousands of lives and millions of dollars in resources.

Every disciple of Christ involved in the great cosmic battle must know that God has established them in spheres where he/she has special authority and responsibility under the Kingdom. Each one is set in a "province" of time of unique opportunity, but beyond which he or she is increasingly ineffective. It is of great importance to "seize the time," but also to recognize when that sphere of time is past. One's failure to grasp his *kairos* period may mean missing out on what God is doing in that moment, but failure to recognize the passing of that time may result in the quenching of a new level of God's activity. There are those in the history of the Church who were used mightily to advance the Kingdom in their hour but attempted to hold on after their time was over. They measured the new move of God against the standard of the old, became critical, and in some cases became quenchers of revival themselves.

Christ's people in the cosmic battle are also established in a particular place. In Joshua 1:3, God tells Joshua, who is at *his* time and place, "Every place on which the sole of your foot treads, I have given it to you, just as I spoke to Moses." This same promise applies to the true Church. The very land she occupies has been set apart for the Kingdom. The true Church has penetrated the zone of occupation, and she has established there an outpost in the midst of the land claimed by the enemy.

What is the true Church? Jesus told Simon Peter, "And I also say to you that you are Peter, and upon this rock I will build My church; and the gates of Hades shall not overpower it."[12]

First, the true Church is built upon the "rock" of Jesus Christ. Simon is *Petros*, a "piece" of rock, not the whole stone. Jesus Himself is the Rock. Jesus said in Luke 20:17, "...What then is this that is written, 'The stone which the builders rejected, this became the chief corner stone'?" Even the Old Testament pointed to Christ as the Rock. As the Hebrews plodded through the Sinai, they "...all drank the same spiritual drink, for they were drinking from a spiritual rock which followed them; and the rock was Christ."[13]

12. Matthew 16:18.
13. 1 Corinthians 10:4.

Therefore, the Church Jesus builds is one established on Him. That church has one passion—to know Jesus and to obey Him.

Second, the true Church is not stopped by the gates of hell. The "gates" are the portals representing authority. The power of the kingdom of darkness cannot withstand the Church Jesus builds. Such a church is recognized by its aggressiveness and penetration of the enemy's stronghold. It reaches into zones of authority within its city, such as areas of political corruption, sexual perversion and abuse, and regions of injustice, making disciples of people held in bondage there. Such a church also reaches its "own kind," as well, but it is not limited by that. The Jesus-built church is recognizable because it is on the prophetic cutting edge, populated by all types of people.

A third sphere exists for the people of God—that of function. God sets individuals and churches into specific functions determined by call, gift, and anointing. The call is the command to a certain ministry. Gifting makes available the resources necessary to implement the call. Anointing empowers the gifted ones to use the gifts effectively and dynamically. Understanding one's function in the Kingdom involves discerning one's call, gifts, and points of effectiveness.

Understanding the significance of ministry of place produces both boldness and humility. Boldness comes with the recognition of one's authority in a given area, humility with the knowledge that it is an area of limited scope. This is what Paul means when he says:

For we are not overextending ourselves, as if we did not reach to you, for we were the first to come even as far as you in the gospel of Christ; not boasting beyond our measure, that is, in other men's labors, but with the hope that as your faith grows, we shall be, within our sphere, enlarged even more by you, so as to preach the gospel even to the regions beyond you, and not to boast in what has been accomplished in the sphere of another (2 Corinthians 10:14-16).

There is great power and authority for the man or woman who operates in the particular place of space and time that God has given them. How does one find that place? The answer lies in abandoning oneself to the Lordship of Christ. Jesus was always in the right place at the right time. He was always in His "sphere" because His passion was to do the Father's will. He sought to do only what the Father did, not taking His own initiative, but carefully seeking the Father's direction.[14] Such commitment requires intense intimacy and communion with "headquarters." The person who yearns to do the will of God regardless of the cost, and who devotes time to intimacy with God, never has to fret about finding his or her place. Such persons will find themselves there, not because they have arranged, manipulated, pulled strings, or maneuvered, but because they are abandoned to the Father's will.

The sphere of authority will also determine the method of fighting the war. Tragically, too often the Church has

14. See John 5.

not understood this. A segment of the Church has reacted to the fierce issues of the late twentieth century with what has been termed "assault Christianity." A vigorous facet of the Church began getting into society's face, going nose to nose against abortion advocates, militant homosexuals, pompous media elites, even the President of the United States. "Getting into someone's face" is an expression for speaking the truth head-on. It is an historic and legitimate ministry of the Church of Jesus Christ. Getting into society's face is the Church raising her prophetic voice, calling culture to holiness. But it is not "assault Christianity."

The prophets of Israel were good at getting into society's face—the right way. Amos was certainly in the face of Israel's pampered class when he called their women "cows of Bashan." Jeremiah went eyeball to eyeball with false prophets when he warned of impending captivity, to the irritation of popular opinion. Jesus was constantly in the face of self-exalting dead religion. No one will ever match the way the Lord went head to head against the devil on the cross. And if the Church is the Body of Christ, she ought to do what He did in His body. The Church ought to be in the face of everything hellish in culture—but in the *right way*.

A militant church is always in danger of becoming, in philosophy and strategy, exactly like her enemy. Its passion turns to hatred. It becomes increasingly aggressive, and out of that heat uses ever stronger tactics until at last it is making bombs, stowing up guns, and preparing to kill and maim.

How does the Church get in society's face without succumbing to the mentality of anger-driven militancy?

The key is to start with the character of God, as revealed in Jesus. God's purpose for creation is to fill it with His life and love. Love is meaningless without choice, but choice is meaningless without freedom. God gives us the choices, then provides the freedom through which choice can be made.

Freedom means people have the right to choose, including making wrong choices. Even God will not force people into truth. Men and women have to respond freely to His invitation. One has to win the right to get into someone's face and still respect that person's God-given freedom to choose lifestyle and behavior. God won the right to get into humanity's face at the cross. When a church understands this and acts on it, its militancy becomes redemptive and healing. When it doesn't, it looks no different from any other crusading organization and does far more wounding than healing.

So how do our churches win the right to get into society's face? Jesus won that right by being a servant, and He instructed His followers to do the same.[15] The Church, then, wins the right to speak head-on to her culture by being a servant, not a mean-spirited crusader.

As repugnant as it may sound to some, if the Church wants to get in the face of homosexuals, she must first wash the feet of homosexuals. The Church *should* be in the face of the monstrous practice of abortion on demand. She wins the right to do this when she cares for unwed

15. See Matthew 20.

mothers and their babies, when she helps heal those who have had abortions and bears their spiritual and emotional scars.

Alex was up front with me from the first day we had a detailed conversation. "I test HIV-positive," he said. AIDS had not yet manifested in him, though he carried its seed in his body. Alex, a peppery Louisiana Cajun, had been a practicing homosexual. Then he had been touched by Jesus and changed. His wife sat with him as he talked with me that day.

Alex's dream was to launch a ministry that would serve people sick with AIDS. It would be called "Positive Christians." He wanted to know if I, as his pastor, would give my blessing to such a work and encourage our church to stand with him. He looked at me with all the piercing intensity of Cajun eyes, and asked, "Will you be willing to go into the baptismal waters with people who have AIDS?"

Suddenly I understood the relevance of Mark 16:17-18, where Jesus said,

> *And these signs will follow those who have believed: in My name they will cast out demons; they will speak with new tongues; they will pick up serpents, and if they drink any deadly poison, it shall not hurt them; they will lay hands on the sick, and they will recover.*

Scholars have debated whether that "ending" of Mark is part of the original Gospel. I suddenly knew it was an authentic word for the hour in which the Kingdom Church will walk.

"Yes," I answered.

In the years that followed, God held off the advance of AIDS from Alex. Doctors looked at him and predicted that he would be dead in six months, but Alex lived on. The ministry was conceived, gestated, then began to take infant steps. Our church watched Alex and his wife Leigh Ann minister to AIDS patients. They washed their clothes, changed their sheets, emptied their bedpans, drove them to the doctor, and arranged their funerals.

The fire never left Alex. He came to hate the demons that snared men into the homosexual lifestyle. Alex became an ardent spokesman against homosexuality, risking retribution from the increasingly militant homosexual community. But he never stopped loving the human beings. Because he was a servant to them, he had the right to get into their face about their lifestyle. Many of them listened and heard. Ultimately, AIDS snuffed out Alex's earthly life, but not before the courageous little man had raided the enemy's house and rescued a number of people who, like him, were at death's threshold.

In that same period, I heard a young activist for another cause say that, "Christians are tired of being stepped on." It must be noted that servants usually get stepped on. The question Jesus posed to His disciples 2,000 years ago still applies today: If the Master of the Church is persecuted, why should His followers be surprised when it happens to them? The call to the Church is to be like the Lord of the Church—a servant, even to the point of laying down one's life. Every church who learns this will have won the right to get into society's face, as Alex did. Such a church will not have to raise its voice because people will listen.

Increasingly, as the emerging Church walks in her fresh strategy, society will take note.

That strategy is called *militant love.* Jesus defines it, as recorded in Matthew 5:43-46:

> *You have heard that it was said, "You shall love your neighbor, and hate your enemy." But I say to you, love your enemies, and pray for those who persecute you in order that you may be sons of your Father who is in heaven; for He causes His sun to rise on the evil and the good, and sends rain on the righteous and the unrighteous. For if you love those who love you, what reward have you? Do not even the tax gatherers do the same?*

Saul of Tarsus knew a great deal about "assault religion." He likely would have scorned the suggestion that he should love his enemies. Yet, under the transforming touch of Jesus, Saul is changed into the Paul who writes, "the love of Christ compels us."[16] To be a follower of Jesus is to be motivated by His love, even when confronting the evil in society and those human beings who advance it.

Assault Christianity is one institution besieging other institutions, one arsenal of ideas seeking to outgun other arsenals of ideas. Militant love is life attacking death, light coming against darkness, truth colliding with lies.

Jesus demonstrated the characteristics of militant love. First, it produces the positive stroke, not the negative. Once Jesus was journeying from Galilee to Jerusalem. The best route would take Him through Samaria. Because of

16. 2 Corinthians 5:14 NKJ.

tensions with the Jews, Jesus sent His disciples to the region to see if the Samaritans would receive Him. The Samaritans refused, and James and John asked Jesus, "Lord, do You want us to command fire to come down from heaven and consume them?" Jesus rebuked His disciples, and said, "You do not know what manner of spirit you are of, for the Son of Man did not come to destroy men's lives, but to save them."[17]

Jesus shows that militant love does not inflict suffering on others, but is willing to receive it on itself for the sake of others. Militant love does not nail its enemies to the cross, but goes to the cross on behalf of the enemy. Militant love blesses those who curse it, does good to those who hate it, and prays for those who spitefully use and persecute it.[18] Militant love does aggressive acts of kindness toward those who cause it hurt. It washes the feet of those who would betray it.

In defining militant love, Jesus says in Luke 6:35, "...love your enemies, and do good, and lend, expecting nothing in return; and your reward will be great, and you will be sons of the Most High; for He Himself is kind to ungrateful and evil men." The follower of Christ is to love his or her enemies aggressively. Love, by this definition, is something one chooses to do whether he or she feels it or not.

How do we show love toward our enemies? Jesus said that one way is for us to bless those who curse us. Blessing

17. See Luke 9:52-56.
18. See Luke 6:27-28.

a person means to speak good things upon him or her. The Bible sees blessing someone as an act that sets in motion a flow of good toward the person to whom it's spoken. When we bless someone, we become co-laborers with God, His mouthpiece in launching that flow of good toward a person. It's easy enough to speak this on our families and friends, but Jesus calls on us to speak this on those with a hostile state of mind toward us. In the dynamics of the Kingdom of God, the action of cursing spoken toward us should cause the reaction of blessing from us, through the Spirit of God. Perhaps this even erects a barrier against the curse aimed at us. This seems to be the point made in Proverbs 15:1, which says, "A gentle answer turns away wrath, but a harsh word stirs up anger." And Proverbs 26:2 says, "Like a sparrow in its flitting, like a swallow in its flying, so a curse without cause shall not alight."

Once, a teacher was repairing his concrete driveway. Just as he sat to rest, he saw a child putting his handprint in the wet concrete. The teacher rushed over and grabbed the youngster and was about to spank him. The teacher's neighbor saw this and said, "Don't you remember? You must 'love' the child, not punish him."

The teacher replied, "I do love him in the abstract, but not in the concrete."

Many of us love people in the abstract, even our enemies. But Jesus says we are to do concrete things toward our enemies that demonstrate the attitude of love. This is aggressive, open, militant love. It is also another way in which the evil intent of the enemy's heart is deflected, as Proverbs 25:21-22 shows:

If your enemy is hungry, give him food to eat; and if he is thirsty, give him water to drink; for so you will heap burning coals on his head, and the Lord will reward you.

Further, Jesus specifies militant love by instructing His people to "...pray for those who spitefully use you and persecute you."[19] This means bringing something specific about the enemy to the Lord, asking God to bless the enemy at that particular point.

The power of militant love wins again and again. Some years ago, leaving Kiev, in the former Soviet Union, our team met three young women missionaries at the airport. One was returning to the United States to get married, and the other two had come to see her off. One of these women was a former KGB agent who had stood outside churches and arrested believers under the Communist regime. She had been loved to Christ and had herself become a missionary.

The Christians who ministered to her practiced the same militant love that drove Corrie ten Boom to minister to Germans, even after her sister died in a Nazi concentration camp, and that compelled Elisabeth Elliott to seek to reach the Auca Indians who had murdered her husband Jim.

Militant love identifies the true enemy. Paul writes in Ephesians 6:12:

For our struggle is not against flesh and blood, but against the rulers, against the powers, against the world

19. Matthew 5:44 NKJ.

forces of this darkness, against the spiritual forces of wickedness in the heavenly places.

The Kingdom Church motivated by militant love does not see lost or evil people as the enemy, but as victims of the powers of darkness.

Militant love follows the proper strategy. The Kingdom Church will have a fresh grasp of Second Corinthians 10:4-5, which says,

For the weapons of our warfare are not of the flesh, but divinely powerful for the destruction of fortresses. We are destroying speculations and every lofty thing raised up against the knowledge of God, and we are taking every thought captive to the obedience of Christ.

Thus, the militant love-minded Church does not strike at human beings, who are not the enemy anyway. Rather, she adopts a strategy that utilizes her powerful spiritual weapons. She strikes the real enemy with love-energized truth through her prophetic voice, guided by Spirit-fired discernment, using missiles of heaven-piercing intercession.

All this is punctuated by concrete acts of love, which confuse and disarm her enemies. The Kingdom Church will not surrender her integrity, but neither will she be an instrument of hate.

Chapter 7

Outpost of the Kingdom

When Poland's ambassador to the Soviet Union entered the Kremlin in Moscow on September 22, 1939, he knew what was coming. So when Andre Vishinsky, Deputy People's Commisar for Foreign Affairs, handed him a formal note from the Soviet government, the ambassador refused it. He insisted on knowing what it said first.

"It is a proclamation of the Soviet government that, in view of recent events, the Republic of Poland has ceased to exist," Vishinsky said. Three weeks before, Hitler had invaded Poland, and the country had been brought to its knees. The Soviet Union, in league with the Nazis, stood by like a vulture, ready to pick clean the Polish corpse.

"Poland will never cease to exist!" shot back the ambassador. He adamantly refused to accept the note. The only way the Soviets finally got it into his hands was by sending it to him through the regular mail.

There was no question that the Polish ambassador knew whom he represented.

If Christians are the ambassadors of God's Kingdom, then the true Church that Jesus builds is the "outpost," or "embassy," of the Kingdom of Heaven within the world. One definition of an outpost is "an outlying or frontier settlement." The Church reveals her "outpost" nature in two ways.

First, the church is a "nation within the nations." Philippians 3:20 says that her "citizenship is in heaven." Her involvement with earthly political and governmental systems must always be within the context of that citizenship. She does not belong to, nor do the bidding of any earthly system she may serve. Her "national interests" are totally concentrated on the Kingdom of God. Any involvement in earthly public affairs is for the purpose of serving those Kingdom interests. In Exodus 19:6, God told Israel she was ordained to be a "holy nation." He affirmed this also to the Church in First Peter.

Within every human nation, God establishes His own spiritual nation. Its citizens seek to be the best citizens of their earthly countries precisely because they are citizens of a more noble domain. But the people of God will also be despised at times because they will be doggedly tied to the interests of the Kingdom of God and will not let themselves become enslaved to the narrow interests of the nations where they reside.

The second aspect of the Church's "outpost" nature is that she is an "embassy" of Heaven. Paul writes in Second Corinthians 5:20, "...we are ambassadors for Christ." In modern times, according to *Webster's New Collegiate Dictionary,* an ambassador is "a minister of the highest rank accredited to a foreign government or sovereign as the official representative of his own government or sovereign."[1] Each individual follower of Christ is His "ambassador," and the Church, His "embassy."

There are two critical points here. First, the ambassador represents the nation that sent him and that nation's interests. Second, an ambassador speaks what his sovereign instructs and faithfully represents the very image of his king. When the ambassador speaks, he *is* the voice of the government he represents. The Church must always remember that she represents the Kingdom of God and Kingdom interests. As she addresses those interests on earth, she will find her prophetic voice among the nations.

Occasionally, as a White House aide, I would be dispatched to speak for the President at minor events. Before I departed, I would be given a specific message to deliver. My assignment was to speak all of what I had been given and no more. If I failed to give the message as instructed, I would be called to account when I returned to Washington. I would often begin by saying, "The President has instructed me to tell you...." There would be a hush in the room. There was authority in my representation of the President of the United States. This is why it is so important for the Church to learn to say again, with authority, "Thus says the Lord...." As the outpost of the Kingdom, we are instructed to speak His Word to the nations—all of it, but no more than what God is saying, and certainly no less.

1. *Webster's New Collegiate Dictionary* (Springfield, Massachusetts: G. & C. Merriam Co., 1959).

The most brilliant understanding of this I have heard came from an African diplomat, Jonas Kouassi, who is also a committed Christian. "The situation of an ambassador," he said, "is 'extra-territoriality.' " That is, the nation to which an ambassador is sent must respect the fact that he is "extra-territorial," or comes from outside the territory to which he is sent. This is the basis for diplomatic immunity, where the ambassador is subject to the laws of the nation where he has citizenship, not to the laws of the country where he carries out the embassy function. "The authorities in the countries where we are stationed cannot touch us," Jonas noted. "If we are ambassadors for Christ, we have 'diplomatic immunity,' and the authorities of this world cannot touch us!" As ambassadors of Christ and citizens of the Kingdom of Heaven, the people of God are under "diplomatic immunity" from the powers of hell that temporarily rule over the world. The Kingdom Church is growing in this understanding. As she does, her deeds will increasingly be Kingdom works. And the results will be awesome.

Jonas Kouassi was not referring to civil authority. First Peter 2:13-14 says to Christians:

> *Submit yourselves for the Lord's sake to every human institution, whether to the king as the one in authority, or to governors as sent by him for the punishment of evildoers and the praise of those who do right.*

Jesus tells His followers, in Matthew 22:21, to "...render to Caesar the things that are Caesar's; and to God the things that are God's." Christians are to respect and obey legitimate civil authority as long as such obedience does not cause them to disobey God.

Daniel 2:44 (NKJ) gives this revelation:

And in the days of these kings the God of heaven will set up a kingdom which shall never be destroyed; and that kingdom shall not be left to other people; it shall break in pieces and consume all these kingdoms, and it shall stand forever.

The day will come when God will establish a Kingdom in the earth that will displace all the other kingdoms. When the Kingdom of God comes into the earth, it displaces the kingdom of darkness. When will the Lord manifest this displacement fully in the earth? All we can say is that it will happen after the four symbolic empires have come and gone like a seducer in the night, leaving their offspring, the present world system. Daniel reveals a stone that is carved out and that crushes the world system and becomes a mountain that fills the whole earth. *The stone that is cut out is the Body of the Lord Jesus Christ, the expanding remnant Church, which is the Jesus Church, and therefore the Kingdom Church, the emerging church, and the mountain that fills the earth is the Kingdom itself.*

The Kingdom Church of Jesus Christ is a holy nation, quarried from the nations of men. As she is restored to the fullness of Jesus, her Kingdom works will increase the works of the Kingdom in the earth, crushing the spirit of darkness behind the nations of men.

The increase of Kingdom manifestation will culminate in the Second Coming of the Lord Christ. At that time, the mountain of the Kingdom of God will fill the whole earth, displacing the flimsy kingdoms of this world! In that day, the government will be upon the shoulders of Jesus in operational reality. The culmination of that day comes swiftly, but it is developing now, and has been since the first coming of Jesus, and since Pentecost.

The pattern of this development is seen in parables of Jesus concerning the Kingdom. The principle of growth, like the stone that grows into a mountain that ultimately fills the earth, is illustrated in other ways. Look at Mark 4:26-28:

> *...The kingdom of God is like a man who casts seed upon the soil; and goes to bed at night and gets up by day, and the seed sprouts and grows—how, he himself does not know. The soil produces crops by itself; first the blade, then the head, then the mature grain in the head.*

The emphasis is on inevitability. If the seed is planted and grows, the day will most certainly come when the fruit of the seed, in this case the Kingdom of God, will fully come.

The One who is crucial to all this is the Lord Jesus Christ. He is the Alpha, the point of origination, and the Omega—the destination. Apart from Him, there is no ministry, no coming of the Kingdom in the earth. He is the Seed of the Kingdom, the Planter of the Seed, and the Coming of the Kingdom itself. Wherever He is Lord, the Kingdom is manifest. It is growing now, and it will come in its consummate completeness when He returns. Until then, His Church is the embassy of His Kingdom in this world. As the emerging Church grows in her understanding of this, she will develop mightily in her ability to confront the world system with boldness and effectiveness.

The embassy of the Kingdom of Heaven will not be the slave of any earthly human political system. She will be involved in society and will take a stand on issues. The emerging Church will have one allegiance, one banner—the Kingdom of God—and will understand that, in relation to society's issues, she is the agent of that Kingdom.

In the mid-twentieth century, large segments of the mainline church in America were swept into politics. Issues such as the Civil Rights movement and the Vietnam War energized the churches as they participated in, and sometimes helped plan, marches, demonstrations, and protests. At the same time, the conservative wing of the Church stayed away from this activism, mainly for two reasons. First, many conservative groups believed the institutional church should remain separate from politics; their business was Heaven. Second, conservative churches that had no reservations about political involvement stayed away because they viewed the activism in the Civil Rights-Vietnam era as leftist.

By the late twentieth century, though, the conservative American church was diving into the political waters. The focus had shifted on public issues. Abortion and sexuality were now at center stage. The election of Bill Clinton with his pro-choice abortion and gay rights positions was a bucket of cold water for the conservative evangelicals in the Church, who for decades felt they had the ear of the Presidency. Now it seemed shut to them. Fired by leaders like Pat Robertson, Patrick Buchanan, Oliver North, Beverly LaHaye, Phyllis Schlafley, Ralph Reed and others, conservative churches became intensely active. A Republican sweep in the United States Congress in 1994 encouraged them. For many of them, the Kingdom was being brought into the nation through its political gates.

The Church's voice *must* be heard in the public process. It is true that the United States is in desperate need of spiritual and moral renewal and that the Church of Jesus Christ has the answer. What makes all this so dangerous for the Church is her inadequate understanding of the Kingdom of God. The emerging Church is learning much as she watches and participates in the struggles of the late twentieth century, and this is why she will be different in the next. Her limited concept of the Kingdom, however, makes her vulnerable to becoming little more than an extension of a particular political cause, within the narrow sphere of the national interest of one country. The Church is to represent the interests of the Kingdom of Heaven, not the narrow interests of the particular nation in which she is planted.

Twenty centuries ago, Jesus told His disciples that they didn't understand the Kingdom. He would say the same today. The Church's ignorance at this point can be defined by attitudes that try to limit the Kingdom in any of three ways—temporal, spatial, or ethnic.

Trying to limit the Kingdom spatially produces civil religion, a "national gospel," churches limited in ministry and impact to one component of civilization. But there's also a problem in trying to limit the Kingdom of God to one temporal era. This produces a distorted generationalism. Likewise, to try to lock up the Kingdom in one ethnic group confines it in the chains of culture.

Temporal limitation of the Kingdom of God is the belief that the primary manifestation of the Kingdom of God is restricted to a particular generation within a specific period of time. Rigid dispensationalism rises out of this error. One could say with little problem that God has a variety of ways of dealing with people in different eras. But to say that the scope and power of His works are greater in the confines of one generation—e.g., the "apostolic" period—than in another, is to trap the Kingdom and its works in a particular dispensation and in the generation who happened to be born at that time.

Jesus is the same, yesterday, today, and forever.[2] That simple statement rips apart the tight walls of the cell of temporal entrapment. There is no generation that can say, "the Kingdom belongs more to our time than any other." Neither is there a generation that can believe, "the Kingdom belongs more to the past (or future) generations than to ours."

Spatial limitation believes that the Kingdom of God is ministered primarily in the context of one particular nation to a greater degree than others, and the survival of that nation is linked to the advance of the Kingdom in the world. Catholics and Protestants in Northern Ireland have made the Kingdom of God a spatial issue.

---

2. See Hebrews 13:8.

The same is true with those who are seeking the politicalization of the Church in America. It is as if the agenda is to reform America. Of course, the gospel is reforming in its impact. Of course, it's revolutionary. And America certainly needs spiritual revolution and reformation. But the gospel of the Kingdom of God is not about the United States of America, nor any other spatial entity. It is about a King who alone has the right and authority to rule the nations—whatever they are.

Jesus said it this way,

> *...My kingdom is not of this world. If My kingdom were of this world, then My servants would be fighting, that I might not be delivered up to the Jews; but as it is, My kingdom is not of this realm* (John 18:36).

Ethnic limitation of the Kingdom of God is the idea that the Kingdom belongs essentially to one primary racial group and its culture. The ancient Jews come immediately to mind. They had a hard time receiving the messages proclaimed by Peter and Paul regarding the inclusive heart of God. At various points in American history, southern whites thought they had a lock on the gospel. During the Civil Rights era, there was "Black Theology," which was thought by some to have the edge on understanding God. The British Empire often made little distinction between missions and culturalization. "The white man's burden" meant to some that the aboriginal peoples of various lands had to be hoisted up on the shoulders of Western religion and culture. Much has been written about the cultural entrapment of missions and the barrier it has created against winning non-Westerners to Christ.

"National" churches represent the ethnic and cultural values of the nation where they exist. This is especially true with the various Orthodox churches. In Serbia, for example, the Serbian Orthodox Church takes the position that to be Serbian is to be Orthodox. Non-Orthodox Christians are considered to be a "foreign element" in the land. Orthodox propaganda says that, "The world is against us Serbs and we must stand together and be what we are...and it is the Serbian Orthodox Church that defines what we are." When a church exists primarily to maintain and extend the culture of a particular nation, it ceases to be the agency of the Kingdom of Heaven and becomes the agent of the temporal, human kingdom.

The most recent example of this is in Russia, where the *duma*, or parliament, passed, and President Boris Yeltsin signed, a law proclaiming the Russian Orthodox Church the official church of Russia. The new law prohibits or severely restricts any religious groups that cannot prove that they have been operating in Russia for at least 15 years. The effect of this will be to return religious expression in Russia to conditions similar to those that existed under Communism.

The only way to break loose from the culturalism that is tied to the ethnic entrapment of the Kingdom is to grasp the truth of Galatians 3:28:

> *There is neither Jew nor Greek, there is neither slave nor free man, there is neither male nor female; for you are all one in Christ Jesus.*

The Kingdom of God transcends time, space, and ethnicity. It is bigger than the first century or twentieth, greater in concern than the United States, or Russia, or Palestine, and reaches beyond white Americans, black Africans, or Jewish Israelis. With the pressures on the Church to become a political agency, she must become focused on God's vision for her. The Church of Jesus Christ must realize fully what it means that the purified Church is the agency of the Kingdom of God within the earth.

It is vital that the Church develop a clear theology of the Kingdom. Debate on the true nature of the Kingdom has raged for centuries. Is the Kingdom here now? Will it come only in the future? Can the Church "bring in" the Kingdom? Will it appear at the Second Coming? There are, however, some clear biblical truths that clarify the Kingdom. One is that when Jesus "descended" into the earth, He came in as the seed of the Kingdom. In John 12, certain "Greeks" ask the disciples to show them Jesus. The Lord's followers report the request, and Jesus replies, mysteriously, that the hour has come for Him to be glorified. Then He says to them, "...unless a grain of wheat falls into the ground and dies, it remains by itself alone; but if it dies, it bears much fruit."[3] He is speaking of Himself. The way He will be "seen" is in His disappearance! For as He is "buried," He will be seed that will sprout into abundance of fruit.

The Kingdom, in other words, is in Jesus, and Jesus is in the Kingdom. When Jesus arrives in the earth, the Kingdom arrives, not in its totality or its consummate form, but

3. John 12:24.

it is "seeded" in the world. Seeds develop, grow, and produce fruit. So there's a sequence of Kingdom development already at work in the world, whose full blossoming will inevitably come.

Therefore, the Kingdom is both present now and coming in the future in a greater measure. For 2,000 years, the seed of the Kingdom has been quietly growing. After the initial planting, there is a long period of silence when nothing seems to be happening. The farmer peers out and seems to see nothing. This perhaps is the long period from the ascension of Jesus, through the age of decline and the Dark Ages. The Reformation, perhaps, was the "blade," the first evidence. The Charismatic and Pentecostal renewal may have been the "ear." The restoration to the fullness of Jesus is the full grain of fruit. When that happens, harvest is next! This is because when people see Jesus rather than institutional religion, they come to Him in great numbers, as they did in Galilee and at Pentecost. The world has not seen Jesus on a large scale in 2,000 years. But the day is coming when the Kingdom Church will walk in such purity of His identity, doing the works of the Kingdom, that masses of people will come to Christ.

It should be noted here that *harvest inevitably follows sowing and growing of the seed of the Kingdom.* The emerging Church will be a "harvest church" of immense proportions. In the twentieth century, the Church sought feverishly for growth strategies. Yet the simple truth is that when the Kingdom manifests, there are great ingatherings. Whereas for years, congregations have thought of reaching people in the dozens, or, at most, the hundreds, the emerging Church will see harvests in the thousands, and in some cases, the tens of thousands. This is the major reason that she will have a structural order that reflects that of the New Testament Church. Her outreach will not be limited by the size of her buildings. Rather, she will be a scattered Church, able to reach and disciple the multitudes who will respond to Kingdom ministry.

America is on a collision course with shock and desperation. Many observers are sensing that the nation is moving toward a head-on crash with truth. There is little doubt that a day of hard truth is going to dawn for America when she realizes the horror of her sin. People everywhere will ask: *What have we done? What are we becoming? How can we be saved?*

The hour when nations need the Church more than ever is soon at hand. The Jesus-centered, Spirit-filled, Bible-anchored, Kingdom-ministering Church is potentially the most vital force in society. This is why ungodly authorities have always tried to crush it.

The apostle Paul woke up to this realization. Roger Greenway, in his book, *Apostles to the City*, writes:

> "By revelation (Paul) had come to understand that the church was the long-awaited messianic community, the bearer of the Gospel to all races and nations. It was through the church that God would now fulfill His redemptive purpose for the world."[4]

4. Cited in Floyd McClung, *Seeing the City With the Eyes of God* (Tarrytown, New Jersey: Chosen Books, 1991), 147.

When we truly understand what the Church is, we will no longer be hopeless and despairing about our cities, no longer bored and unexcited about Jesus Christ and His Church.

Individual believers must get a vision of the Church as the Kingdom agency and themselves as Kingdom agents. Societies, including cities, are ruled over by principalities who occupy the ground accumulated through dozens and sometimes hundreds of years of sin. But the power of the Kingdom displaces the demons.

As followers of Jesus see themselves as Kingdom agents and allow God to use them as such, they will displace the powers of darkness in those parts of the city they touch. Every follower of Jesus touches some facet of his or her city. We must get the vision of touching that part—no matter how small—with the Kingdom of God.

Roger Greenway states that when Paul understood the true nature of the Church in its impact on society:

> "The lines of Paul's urban strategy ran from converts, to churches, to the whole Roman society—its governments, institutions and religions. Paul moved out into the highly urbanized Roman world of his day with a definite strategy in mind."[5]

There can be only one objective for the Church of Jesus Christ as it relates to each city: *to minister Jesus to the city.*

Jesus instructed His disciples to pray to the Father, "Thy Kingdom come, Thy will be done, on earth as in

5. McClung, *Seeing the City*, 145.

Heaven...." How does one know when the Kingdom has "come"? The harvest is a certain sign. The Kingdom Church with the Normandy mindset understands that when the supernatural works of the Kingdom are manifest, then the Kingdom has "come" in degree. This is not to say it has come fully, nor that the Church should cease asking the Father for the coming of the Kingdom.

For centuries the Church has sought to be an instrument of *persuasion*. Whenever and wherever the Kingdom "comes," there is a shift in the communication style. John the Baptist, in a dark dungeon, began to wonder about Jesus. He dispatched some of his men to ask Jesus, "Are you really the Messiah?" Jesus' response is recorded in Matthew 11:4-5, "...Go and report to John what you hear and see: the blind receive sight and the lame walk, the lepers are cleansed and the deaf hear, and the dead are raised up, and the poor have the gospel preached to them." This is all because "...the kingdom of God does not consist in words, but in power," says First Corinthians 4:20. "Power," in the Greek here, is *dunamis*, which refers not to an abstraction of power, but to "mighty deeds."

What Jesus was saying to John, and Paul to the Corinthians, was that there was a type of ministry, work, or manifestation that rendered persuasion unnecessary. All that was required was an *explanation* for what people were seeing or experiencing. Whereas the Church has long relied on persuasive powers, ranging from human polemic to brute force, the emerging Church will "announce the Kingdom" as the reason for the mighty displays and works people are observing.

Two dynamics are at work in the present world. The first is the intensification of chaos, evident in deepening spiritual and moral darkness. As humanity comes closer and closer to hell, the pull into darkness is stronger and stronger. The rate of descent accelerates. As the Second Coming of Christ and ensuing judgment approaches, the world becomes more chaotic.

The other dynamic is the purifying of the Church. Jesus, according to Ephesians 5:26, will "cleanse" and "sanctify" His Bride. This does not infer that every church is a "Bride" Church. The identification of the Bride is in Matthew 25, in Jesus' parable of the virgins. Though this may be seen as an illustration of the lack of preparation of persons outside of Christ for His Coming, it is also a powerful picture of a closed church. The virgins shut out of the marriage feast are those without oil. They have lamps, but without the oil, the lamps can't burn.

The Church is engaged in spiritual warfare. She must gear up to a "wartime footing" in order to fight the enemy successfully, just as the British did to defeat Germany in World War II.

In Great Britain, the Prime Minister is not directly elected by the people. He rises to his position because he is the leader of the majority party in Parliament. There is also the monarchy, to whom everything theoretically is submitted. In the 1920s and 30s, Britain enjoyed the same freedoms as any other democratic nation, with ample room for dissent and for people following their own strategies and devices.

When the war broke out, however, the nation had to move to war-footing. It was understood that Churchill would gather a War Cabinet, and that parliamentary dissent would be sharply limited because of the urgency of unity of strategy. Churchill reported to and submitted to his War Cabinet, and all theoretically was submitted to the Crown. Only the King and War Cabinet could challenge Churchill's strategy as war-time Prime Minister. There was virtually no dissent as all rallied to fight the enemy.

Many churches today dissipate the energies needed for Kingdom warfare because of internal disputes that arise because proper biblical government is not in place. The "war cabinet" for a Kingdom church is made up of the five-fold anointings mentioned in Ephesians 4—apostle, prophet, evangelist, pastor, teacher. The apostle is the "prime minister." The prophet is overseer of operations in the war cabinet, making sure that strategies stay true to their plan and goal. The evangelist is concerned with recruiting, bringing in more warriors for the Kingdom. The pastor oversees care for the wounded warriors. The teacher has the great task of making sure the armies are well trained.

All members of this war cabinet submit to the King—Jesus Christ. There is an important responsibility to interact with and listen to the concerns of the troops, but the final decision-making authority rests with the war cabinet, under the King. Thus, churches who still try to mimic secular government styles are not prepared for war.

Oil is a type of the Holy Spirit. A religious institution without the ministry of the Holy Spirit is just that—a religious institution. Because there is no "oil," there is no light in the lamp; hence, such a church can do nothing to resist the darkness in the nation and culture of her residence. It is the Church with both the structure and the oil that undergoes the cleansing of the Bride. She is being prepared to meet the Bridegroom. Many churches today are in turmoil and stress. Although much of it is caused by fallen human beings trying to lead the Church through human flesh, some of it marks the process of cleansing and purifying and should not be resisted but received.

One of the reasons for the huge harvest ahead is that the sparkling beauty being wrought now in the tempest of cleansing in the Church will be in such stark contrast to the profoundly monstrous and ugly world of evil. Desperate people will see in the purified Church an outpost of integrity and righteousness in the wilderness of the chaotic world, and many will rush in.

* * *

The USS *Quincy* cruised into the harbor at Valletta, Malta, on the morning of February 2, 1945, bearing the President of the United States, Franklin Delano Roosevelt. The weather was good, so he sat on the bridge. Out in the distance was the HMS *Orion*. Standing on the deck of the British ship was a familiar figure. Winston Churchill raised his arm and waved at Roosevelt, who signalled his greeting to the Prime Minister.

Suddenly, Spitfires, the perky British fighters that had provided escort, zoomed overhead, as a band struck up the "Star Spangled Banner." Churchill motored over to the

Quincy and lunched with the President. The waters of the harbor were smooth, but the condition of the world the men discussed wasn't.

The immediate goal of the Malta conference was to prepare to meet Joe Stalin days later at Yalta. Roosevelt and Churchill spent hours talking about immediate problems. Once the Nazis were defeated, the future of the globe was still unsettled. Preparations had to be made for "ruling and reigning" in the new order that would follow the final defeat of the oppressor.

The Kingdom Church is being purified ultimately for this same purpose: to "rule and reign" in the new order that will prevail in the world as God's Kingdom is at last fully manifest.

Chapter 8

Assault on the Bunker

On March 7, 1945, the long thrust that had begun on the beaches of Normandy on June 6, 1944, crashed through Hitler's last natural defensive position and into Germany itself. With the capture of the Ludendorff Bridge at Remagen by the Ninth Armored Division, Allied forces funneled into Hitler's territory.

Meanwhile, Patton's Third Army crossed the Rhine at Openheim, and the First Army, at Cologne. Now the Allies snared the Germans in a huge trap. The Ninth Army was north of the Ruhr and plowed eastward. The First Army bolted out of the Remagen bridgehead, striking east and north. On April 1, the two forces met at Paterborn, cutting off the Ruhr. The Fifteenth Army held the west, and units from the First and Ninth swept in, defeating the German defenders in 18 days and taking 300,000 prisoners.

Canadians mopped up the Nazi forces in the Netherlands, and the full force of the Allied powers marched into

Germany as the Soviet forces crossed from the east at Torgau on the Elbe River. Every Allied commander had one target: Berlin, where Hitler was holed up in a bunker with his closest colleagues.

On April 20, 1945, Hitler convened the primary Nazi leaders. Among the topics they discussed was whether Hitler would remain in Berlin or retreat to his "southern Redoubt" in the Bavarian Alps. On April 22, he decided to stay in Berlin.

Once the Russians surrounded Berlin, Hitler was powerless to control anything. On April 29, in the wee hours, the Fuhrer wrote his will. On April 30, after lunch, he shook hands with his mates in the bunker. At 3:30 that afternoon, a shot rang out. Hitler's aides discovered his body stretched out on a sofa, his pistol dangling at his side. Eva Braun, his wife of mere hours, lay dead next to him. As Russian guns thundered nearby, the bodies were carried to the courtyard and burned.

The Third Reich died with Hitler.

This book has sought to demonstrate how the Normandy invasion and its aftermath is a historic type of the invasion and advance of the Kingdom of God in creation. For the occupied universe, Earth is "Normandy" and the field of battle, as Europe was the theater of conquest in the war against Hitler. The events on Planet Earth are as crucial for the whole of the universe as Normandy and the European Theater were for the globe in World War II.

As the Normandy invasion is a type of the First Coming of Jesus, and the ensuing battle a parable of the present, so the final assault on Hitler's bunker is a type of the Second Coming of Christ and the final rout and finish of satan. There is much variation of thought regarding the timing of Christ's Second Coming, the manifestation of the Kingdom in its full scope, and the ultimate overthrow of satan. From the analogy of the final Allied assault on Hitler, a clear picture emerges of the details of Christ's ultimate Kingdom victory.

As Hitler was pushed back to an ever-narrowing strip of territory in the aftermath of the Normandy invasion, so satan is being pushed back now by the forces of the Kingdom of God. For much of the Church, this is a radically new perception. Especially with the arrival of dispensational thinking, many Christians still have the "Dunkirk" mentality. They see the Church as being under assault—being pushed back, with no hope except that of escape.

Earlier, it was mentioned that the Normandy invasion was the symbol of the incarnation of Jesus and that the moment He stepped into the world, satan's defeat was sealed, just as Hitler's was with the arrival of the first Allied troops on European soil. Also, just as Hitler from that day forward progressively lost territory, so the devil has been continually losing ground since the First Coming of Jesus.

Can this be verified? Missiologists like C. Peter Wagner and David Barrett are using modern technology to track the advance of Christ and His Kingdom among the nations. The picture is emerging more clearly than in any previous periods. In the late 1990s, every minute 27 unevangelized people receive a Bible, and 15 a gospel tract. Every 60 seconds 163 people who have never heard the message of Jesus Christ receive the gospel in a context they can understand, with 114 of them accepting Christ. In the century between the 1890s and the 1990s, 5.55 Africans and 5.16 Asians came to Christ every minute. According to Dion Robert, pastor of the 120,000 member Works and Mission Church, Abidjan, Ivory Coast, for every African who converts to Islam, seven receive Christ. From 1986 to 1996, the number of Protestant Christians in Latin America grew from 18.6 million to 59.4 million, a 220 percent increase. This is nine times the growth of the general population. In Africa, 20,000 people are receiving Christ each day. In 1900, three percent of the southern part of Africa was Christian; now, it's almost 60 percent.[1] In 1900, Korea was considered "impossible to penetrate" with the gospel and had no Protestant church. Today, the city of Seoul alone has 7,000 churches, and the nation is 35 percent Christian.[2]

David Barrett chronicles the advance:

- Three hundred sixty five days a year approximately 364,000 people around the world hear the gospel for the first time, with about 70,000 of these accepting Christ.
- At the end of the first century, for every believer in Christ there were 360 unbelievers. Now, there are only seven non-Christians for every Christian.

---

1. *Mission Frontiers Bulletin*, Nov.-Dec. 1996 (Pasadena: U.S. Center for World Missions), 18.
2. *Missions Frontiers Bulletin*, 19.

- Every year, there is a net gain in the world of 44,000 new churches.
- In A.D. 100, there were 12 unreached people groups for every local church. Today, with five million churches globally, there is one unreached people group for every 416 congregations.[3]

So, says George Otis, Jr., "the borders of the unevangelized world have been heaved backward so forcefully that 75 percent of the world's population now have a reasonable opportunity to hear the Gospel...the soldiers of the Lord have now encircled the final strongholds of the serpent."[4]

One of the dynamics making the current campaigns different from those in the past is that many are being launched from territories once regarded as missions frontiers themselves. For example, Latin American churches and mission groups report they are sending teams to 3,000 unreached people groups.[5] The U.S. Center for World Missions notes that "there are currently 60,000 non-Western missions from over 1,000 non-Western mission agencies...serving in places hostile to Western missionaries."[6]

The twentieth century has seen a remarkable acceleration of missions and evangelism. George Otis writes:

---

3. David B. Barrett and Todd Johnson, *Our Globe and How To Reach It* (Birmingham: New Hope, 1990), Global Diagram 12, 25. Cited in George Otis, Jr., *The Last of the Giants* (Tarrytown: Fleming H. Revell/Chosen Books, 1991), 145.
4. Otis, *Last of the Giants*, 144.
5. *Missions Frontiers Bulletin*, 18.
6. *Mission Frontiers Bulletin*, 18.

> "Of the 788 known global plans for world evangelization conceived by the Church since the issuance of the Great Commission, 540, or nearly seventy percent of them, were birthed subsequent to 1900. In the thirty-year span from 1961 to 1991 alone, the tally of new worldwide plans more than tripled the number launched during the first 1,500 years of Church history."[7]

The World War II invasion of Germany, then, seems an accurate illustration of the advance of the Kingdom prior to Christ's return. As the statistics indicate, and as history shows, it is not unreasonable to expect that close to the Lord's Second Coming, satan's stronghold may be reduced to a tiny sliver of territory.

This is not to suggest that evil fades away. Jesus Himself says the tares will grow right along with the wheat. For too long, though, the Church has focused more on the increase of evil than on the advance of the Kingdom. Evil will not be plucked from the world totally until Christ is enthroned as Lord-in-fact as well as Lord *de jure*. There is no doubt that the Church should be encouraged and keep pressing forward. The enemy's bunker is in sight!

The final assault on the enemy and his ultimate destruction will occur at Christ's Second Coming. In the meantime, as God's Kingdom advances, satan's territory will shrink. The Scripture indicates that the renewed Church will greatly advance the Kingdom. This is what Jesus meant

7. *Mission Frontiers Bulletin*, 144.

when He said that the gospel of the Kingdom would be preached to all the nations before the "end" comes.

Matthew 13:37-43 makes a clear linkage between the advance of the Kingdom in the earth and the return of Christ:

> *And He answered and said, "The one who sows the good seed is the Son of Man, and the field is the world; and as for the good seed, these are the sons of the kingdom; and the tares are the sons of the evil one; and the enemy who sowed them is the devil, and the harvest is the end of the age; and the reapers are angels. Therefore just as the tares are gathered up and burned with fire, so shall it be at the end of the age. The Son of Man will send forth His angels, and they will gather out of His kingdom all stumbling blocks, and those who commit lawlessness, and will cast them into the furnace of fire; in that place there shall be weeping and gnashing of teeth. Then the righteous will shine forth as the sun in the kingdom of their Father. He who has ears, let him hear.*

After Hitler's defeat, the Allied powers established a new order in Germany. In fact, Churchill and other Allied leaders had long been planning for the occupation of German territory. As early as the summer of 1943, Clement Atlee, under Churchill's direction, had proposed to the Americans and Soviets a plan of occupation. "At this time," said Churchill, "the subject seemed purely theoretical. No one could foresee when or how the end of the war would come."[8]

---

8. Winston Churchill, *Memoirs of the Second World War* (Boston: Houghton Mifflin Company, 1987), 958.

The point is, Churchill and the others were looking ahead to victory. The Church must learn this lesson. As she focuses on the war, she must also plan for the season of her reigning and ruling as the agency of the Kingdom of God in the earth.

There were positive aims in the establishment of the new order for Germany. In speaking to the British people, Churchill warned that the "honorable purposes" for which Britain had gone to war against Hitler not be forgotten. These aims, he said, were described by the words, *freedom*, *democracy*, and *liberation*. He called for the establishment of law and justice.

In a far grander sense, these are the aims God will achieve in His Kingdom order within the earth and outward into all creation. Through Christ, He has established freedom and is now using the advancing Church to win the world's liberation. "Democracy" is, of course, the rule of the people. From the beginning, God has gifted people with soul-freedom. But true self-rule is possible only under theocratic rule. When God rules in the individual heart and over human affairs, there is the purest "democracy." God's righteousness is the determinant and standard of His Law and justice. The Kingdom of God is the rule of the character of God. In the order of the Kingdom, God's cosmos will replace the enemy's chaos, because Kingdom order is established on the law and justice inherent in God's holy character.

The order of this Kingdom can be observed in two ways. The first is to see it "in isolation," apart from creation. The other is to view it in terms of its impact on fallen creation.

Three characteristics defining the nature of God's Kingdom are revealed in John 17. The Kingdom of God is personal and relational; it is the realm of glory; and it is the Kingdom of love.

When Jesus prays in John 17, several times He speaks of His "with-ness" in relation to the Father. The Father and Son, with the Holy Spirit, are in relationship. The Kingdom of God is not an impersonal domain presided over by an uncaring ruler. At the heart of God's Kingdom is relationship—intimacy.

In contrast, the fallen human kingdom, as seen in Huxley's *Brave New World*, or Orwell's *1984*, views human beings as machines to be manipulated for the ends determined by the power elites and destroyed if and when they cannot meet those ends. Abortion is on one end of that continuum and euthanasia on the other. In that twisted realm, man, in the description of Buckminster Fuller, is

> "...a self-balancing , 28-jointed adaptor-based biped, and electro-chemical reduction plant, integral with the segregated stowages of special energy extracts in storage batteries, for subsequent actuation of thousands of hydraulic and pneumatic pumps, with motors attached...."

This is the view of the techno-kingdom, in which relationship is unnecessary, and may even be an obstacle to progress.

If the Kingdom of God is relational, in contrast to the foregoing view, it must also be personal. Personalities intertwine in the Kingdom of God, so much so that Father,

Son, and Holy Spirit are one. Therefore, respect and sensitivity mark the Kingdom of God.

The Kingdom of God is the realm of glory. Jesus prayed, "And now, O Father, glorify Me together with Yourself, with the *glory* which I had with You before the world was."[9] The Greek word *doxa*, or glory, carries the thought of value and worth. Thus, the Kingdom of God is the Kingdom of supreme value. It is the "pearl of great price" that one should sell everything to get.[10] The Kingdom of God stands in contrast to the fallen kingdom, which is tawdry and cheap in comparison.

Doxa also means honor. Honesty and integrity are marks of the Kingdom of glory. This is neither stern artificial pietism nor smug religious pride. It is the radiance of pure character, the sum total of the attributes of God. Fallen humanity echoes the sad confession of Adam, "I was...afraid."[11] But the hope of glory is Christ within people. He is the fulness of the Father, character and all. This hope is not a vague wish for improvement. It is a hope in actuality. Human beings, through their identification with Christ, become "partakers of the divine nature."[12]

The Kingdom of God is also the Kingdom of love. In John 17:24 Jesus said,

9. John 17:5 NKJ, emphasis added.
10. Lewis Mumford, *The Myth of the Machine*, (New York: Harcourt Brace, 1970), 56.
11. See Genesis 3:9-10
12. 2 Peter 1:4.

> *Father, I desire that they also, whom Thou hast given Me, be with Me where I am, in order that they may behold My glory, which Thou hast given Me; for* ***Thou didst love Me before the foundation of the world.*** [13]

Two things are evident here. First, love is eternal, preceding creation; and it is the core of the relationships in the Kingdom of God. It is the compelling force behind the fellowship of the Kingdom. In the fallen world of the Babylonian world system, relationships are conditional, based on one party's ability to meet the desires of another. This is equivalent to prostitution. Prostitution is not love. Standing in brilliant contrast is the love at the heart of the Kingdom of God. It is from this that humanity has fallen.

Second, the Kingdom of love reflects the heart of God, that the created realm would enter into the love at the core of the Kingdom. In John 17:26 Jesus prays, "And I have made Thy name known to them, and will make it known; that the love wherewith Thou didst love Me may be in them, and I in them."

As noted earlier, the created order was made as a vessel to be filled with God's glory. Genesis 1 records that God saw that all that He had made was "good." The Hebrew word for "good" means "that which is pleasant and delightful," but it also has the deeper meaning of bringing delight in the heart of someone who looks with pleasure on that which He loves. God is pleased with His creation because He loves it and because it will benefit those He loves. Thus, it is a crucible, filled with His love.

---

13. Emphasis added.

It is noteworthy that God does not pronounce His created order *very* good until after He has created man as *male and female.* Now two beings are joined who can enter into the physical expression of the communion of love, which God poured into His creation. That's what makes the world *very* good.

The Greek word *hamartia,* or "sin," literally means "to miss the mark." It is not simply the idea of the arrow veering to the right or left of the bull's-eye, but it also carries the notion of the missile falling short of the target. To sin, says Romans 3:23, is to "fall short of the glory of God." The glory is seen in the order of the Kingdom, and humanity is falling away from, coming short of this Realm, whose glory and order are established in the person and character of God. This is the essence of the plunge into chaos, as creation is sucked into the vortex.

There was a specific event in pre-creation eternity that precipitated the downward spiral of spiritual gravity. It was referred to earlier as the "lucifer event." After lucifer's fall, in human time at least, God created the universe as we know it, designing it as a crucible to receive His love. At first, there was perfection, and the ideal was realized. Because man was perfectly joined to God, he was in perfect relation with himself, the other person in his life, and with nature. But love mandates choice. When man chose sin, he was broken off from God and began his plunge into chaos. The results were immediate: Adam was now broken off from himself; from Eve, the other person in his life; and from nature.

When man sins, he pulls close to satan, identifies with satan's evil, and becomes caught in his destiny, which is the "pit." God has given man dominion over natural creation. What human beings choose for the world is what will take place. Therefore, because of the choice of Adam, "creation was subjected to futility" and is in bondage to corruption.[14]

The evidence of this descent into chaos is everywhere—from the aging that takes place in the human body to the Second Law of Thermodynamics, which states that physical nature tends to move from order to disorder. The decay strikes at society, and there is increasing chaos in human relations, because lucifer makes "the earth tremble," "shakes kingdoms," makes "the world as a wilderness," and "destroys its cities."[15]

Chaos reigns in the social realm as well. It disorders individuals, families, and society, resulting in chaos in the nations.

The good news is that God has come to make rescue possible. He entered human history in the person of Jesus Christ, subjecting Himself to the vortex at the physical level. He identifies with human beings caught in the tug of spiritual gravity, feels all its fury, but is not corrupted by it.[16] In the midst of the terrifying path to hell, God builds a bridge. All who take it cross over from chaos to cosmos. The bridge is the cross of Jesus Christ.

14. Romans 8:20.
15. Isaiah 14:16-17.
16. Hebrews 4:15.

The very moment a person takes that span, he or she is restored to the Kingdom of God in fact. The individual becomes a new creation, with a new father, set into a new family and a new nation that is not sliding toward the pit with lucifer. This is *justification.*

Throughout life, as long as he or she submits to the Lordship of Jesus Christ, the person walking in Christ, through His Spirit, becomes Christlike. This is *sanctification.*

At the end of time, when Christ returns for that person and all others who follow Him, the individual in Christ receives a new body, one not pulled into the vortex of chaos and deterioration. This is *glorification.*

The entry of Christ into the frightening zone of chaos set up a different force in the universe. It is the reverse of spiritual gravity, the termination of the journey toward hell for all who will receive it. Christ becomes the second Adam. In the first Adam, all is identified with lucifer and his destiny. In the second Adam, all who choose can be identified with Jesus—the perfect righteousness of the Father—and with His destiny. Everyone is either plunging with lucifer or rising with Jesus. For though the plunge into chaos and the pit goes on for the world identified with lucifer, there is now another dynamic at work in those identified with Christ—the very reversal of chaos! This is the truth of Second Corinthians 3:18:

> *But we all, with unveiled face beholding as in a mirror the glory of the Lord, are being transformed into the same image from glory to glory, just as from the Lord, the Spirit.*

It's also the good news of Second Corinthians 4:16:

Therefore we do not lose heart, but though our outer man is decaying, yet our inner man is being renewed day by day.

Everything Jesus touches He puts into order. The order of Jesus is the expression of the Kingdom of God. People disordered by overt demonization come to Him, He delivers them, and tells people, "But if I cast out demons with the finger of God, then the kingdom of God has come upon you."[17] He touches the disordering of human bodies ravaged by sickness, sets them in order (this is called "healing"), and proclaims the Kingdom. In fact, the sweeping Greek word for salvation, *sozo*, doesn't refer merely to salvation for eternal life, but to healing, deliverance, and total rescue from the dominion of darkness.

This, then, is the hope of the nations. Followers of Jesus Christ should not despair. It is true that evil is on the rise. It is, sadly, a fact that the plunge into chaos is speeding up. But the people of God must fix their minds on the fact that the Kingdom of God arrived in the Lord Jesus Christ, and although the fallen kingdom tumbles downward at an alarming rate, the Kingdom of God is increasing with determined, unstoppable force toward the bunker, the last redoubt of the enemy of creation.

* * *

Reutlingen is a jewel of a city, glittering in the tiara of the Stuttgart region. In the mid-twentieth century, like the rest of Germany, the Nazis occupied it and turned its human

17. Luke 11:20.

and material resources to their demonic cause. But a half century later, a visitor from another planet would scarcely guess that Reutlingen's shining facets had been dirtied by the Nazi reign.

On any given day in the 1990s, Frau Ruth Koch goes about her routine. She sings as she works, and one who draws close can hear that the words are those of praise to God. Her husband, Herbert, early in the morning, takes his highly-marked Bible from a near-by table and probes deep into its treasures. The Kochs pray for their sons, one a pastor, another a leader in a church in far-away Australia, yet another an engineer living not far from Reutlingen.

One would never know the horror inscribed in the memory banks of Herbert and Ruth Koch's minds. The joy and peace of Christ have displaced the Nazi monstrosities they lived through.

Nor would one guess that the area where they live had ever heard the thunder of Hitler's jackboots resounding through the valley. A friend of the Kochs, Johann Eberhardt, leaves his comfortable home in Metzingen, just miles from Reutlingen, on his rounds as a technician for Kodak. He drives a route through a serene spread of gentle hills dressed in the coat of many-colored grape and cherry orchards.

The thump of guns and bombs and raspy-throated "*Sieg Heil!*" voices belonged to another world, one which has been dead these 50-plus years. As Johann calls on his customers, all this is routine to him and he hardly reflects on the fact that Germany, on the eve of the twenty-first century, thrives under the new order established following the conquest of Hitler.

This new Germany is as much a natural type of spiritual realities as the Nomandy invasion. For the occupied world, through the advance of Christ's Kingdom, is moving to an era in which the occupation of the oppressor is as much a thing of the dim past as Hitler's domination of Germany is now.

In the before-time, the angelic order was made to rule over God's creation. It was assigned territories and regions to serve as the messengers of God. However, a third of the angels fell with lucifer. God speaks to the fallen angels, "I said, 'You are gods, and all of you are sons of the Most High. Nevertheless you will die like men, and fall like any one of the princes.' "[18] Then God raised up human beings, created in His image, to take dominion over the world. Of this creature, the Holy Spirit reveals:

> *Yet Thou hast made him a little lower than God, and dost crown him with glory and majesty! Thou dost make him to rule over the works of Thy hands; Thou has put all things under his feet, all sheep and oxen, and also the beasts of the field, the birds of the heavens, and the fish of the sea, whatever passes through the paths of the seas. O Lord, our Lord, how majestic is Thy name in all the earth!* (Psalm 8:5-9)

As we have said, whatever has dominion over man will determine how man exercises the dominion God gives

18. Psalm 82:6-7.

him. What is happening in the Church in the closing years of the twentieth century is the move of God, establishing His dominion over human beings who belong to Him. For those people are destined to rule and reign in the new world that will emerge when the occupier is at last driven out totally, and the occupied planet is liberated—down to its last piece of territory.

END